HOLY
LAUGHTER!

Humor in the Bible

The Dean James Version

Holy Laughter! Humor in the Bible
Copyright © 2011 by The Dean James Version.
All rights reserved.

ISBN-13: 978-1461067351
ISBN-10: 1461067359

Cover Art: "Laugh Eternal" © 2010 by The Dean James Version.

TABLE OF CONTENTS

Thanks A Lot!

The Big Intro

The Ancient Testament

The Not As Ancient Testament

Parting Thoughts

Author's Note:

When I use someone else's material, I cite the source; or say "Author Unknown"; or an "old joke". I hope you enjoy what I wrote and want to tell your friends. Please quote me and be sure to mention my book. I need the **free publicity**; and I don't want my work deemed "Author Unknown".

Blessings & Joy,

The Dean James Version

THANKS A LOT!

The Apostle Paul told the Thessalonians to give thanks in everything, so here I go.

Thank You God for making me, blessing me, and providing me with all this great material! Without His Holy Word, this book would merely be: "Laughter! Humor in the"

Thanks to Amy Sell for her offbeat sense of humor and encouragement.

Thanks to my parents for raising me with a sense of humor. Thanks to my brother Richard, sister Lisa, sister-in-law Sharon, brother-in-law Larry, and my wonderful nieces Laura, Dana, Reagan, and Parker. Thanks to my aunts, uncles, cousins, etc. who exude comedy of all sorts at our family get-togethers.

Thanks to Cindy Byrnes O'Halloran for her fantastic feedback. Thanks to Josh Sitta for helping my drawing appear more vibrant and less Etch-A-Sketchy. And thanks to Mike Cotton of Cotton Web Design for his insightful assistance too.

Thanks to all my fun and funny friends, especially the Dittmers. Omar (Hey O!) & Gladys. Greg & Jenny; Joel & Marci; David & Amy; Janice. And all their children! Pastor David & Sandra Lingard who rescued me when my appendix burst!

Thanks to the family of believers at St. Paul Lutheran Church! Pastor Ron & Barb Pennekamp. And everyone else. (Too many to name!)

Posthumous thanks goes to my Grandpa Eddie Johnston who read and lived the Bible and always offered a friendly smile, a jovial laugh, a funny joke, prayers, encouragement, kind words, and candy: Smarties and Bazooka Joe Bubble Gum.

I also offer fond remembrances of my cousin Lon Adams who exhibited a hearty sense of humor; my cousin Laura Dunn who had a fun laugh; and much thanks to Barb Fecht who led the youth group and let me cut up.

And thank you, yes you, for reading this book! May you be blessed in wonderful ways for allowing me to share this labor of love and joy with you. More thanks if you paid for the book.

Especially full price!

Even more thanks if you buy several more copies to give as gifts. Birthdays, Christmas, Easter, anytime!

And while you're being so generous,
please support:

World Vision
http://donate.worldvision.org

Thank you again.
May you be blessed to be a blessing.
Laughter & Love in the LORD!

Your blessed buddy,
Dean

THE BIG INTRO

Finding humor in the Bible's not as daunting as it sounds; because inside Scripture, laughter abounds. Why? God has a sense of humor! If you doubt that, look at your relatives. Everyone has at least one funny uncle, knows of someone who does, or is one.

Do other religions have sacred texts with intentional humor? I'm not suggesting the Bible is a book of humor. But God is a Being of Joy. The Gospel is The Good News!

I hope you like old jokes. Jokes as old as the Bible. God's jokes! Divine Comedy. If you choose not to laugh, that's your choice. I for one would reconsider. Especially during thunderstorms. And I hope you enjoy new jokes too. My jokes!

Although the words comedy, humor, funny, and joke do not appear in the NKJV Bible, the word laugh appears 108 times. Oh sure, 76 of those times, it appears as part of the word slaughter, but it still appears. And that still leaves 32 times for the words laugh, laughs, or laughter.

Proverbs 17:22a (NKJV):
A merry heart does good,
like medicine.

Proverbs 15:15b (NASB):
But a cheerful heart
has a continual feast.

Questions to Ponder:

● Which animal did Christian musician David Meece call "the original Mister Ed"?

● Who said (in the RSV): "Do I lack madmen, that you have brought this fellow to play the madman in my presence?"

● Which book of the Bible do I say is like a textbook on how to write a great comedy?

● What's so funny about a handkerchief?

And more importantly:

● What makes a great gift for birthdays, confirmation, Easter, Thanksgiving, Christmas, anytime?

● Play "The Crosscheck Cookie Game!" Whenever you find a wordplay with the word cross in Holy Laughter! Humor in the Bible: Eat a cookie.
… Or to be more fun: Eat a hot cross bun.
… Or to be healthy, a carrot.

The answers can be found as you read along.

Enjoy!

And may God bless you!
Even when you don't sneeze.

THE ANCIENT TESTAMENT

<u>GENESIS</u>

Jenny says, I mean, Genesis means the beginning. This is our origin story. Who we are as humanity; and how we came to be. Or rather, how we got ourselves into this mess.

From the very beginning, we've never been able to stick to a diet. Even the simplest of diets, where you can eat anything and everything you want, except one thing. So what do we do? We eat that one thing.

And how odd mankind got kicked out of Paradise for eating the forbidden fruit, 'cause nowadays, so few of us eat enough produce.

Funny Critters

Genesis 1:24

God creates all the animals of the Earth! That includes the platypus, chimpanzee, kangaroo, and giraffe! Our funny uncles. That one neighbor who always washes his car when it rains.

These creatures, and more, certainly show God has a sense of humor. Especially penguins when they waddle and slide on the ice. Good, clean fun. Unless they become rabid and attack. And then, not so much.

The Blame Game

Genesis 3:1-13

When Adam and Eve sin, they blame others! So in Adam's eyes, it wasn't his fault. It was God and Eve's! Even Eve blames the serpent. "He tricked me!"

Notice Adam's audacity! "The woman whom <u>You</u> made to be with me." (<u>Emphasis</u> added.) In other words, "It's all Your fault, God. If You hadn't made that snake-following, forbidden-fruit-eating woman, none of this would have happened! I'd still have my rib; humanity would still have its dignity; and I could still go commando."

**How could Paradise be Paradise
if It had snakes?**

Morris Goodwin
from New Zealand told me:
"The snake had to tempt Eve,
'cause Adam would've killed it with a shovel."

**Although the Bible never specifies,
most folks claim
the forbidden fruit was an apple,
but I think it was a banana.
Because in my experience,
forbidden fruit always comes in bunches.
And has appeal.**

Amy Sell says that after Cain killed Abel, Adam griped, "What's with the kids these days? Why, when I was their age, I was dirt!"

**Noah saved all his pennies
for the Great Flood.**

Noah financed the building of the ark with several small monthly payments, culminating in a huge umbrella payment.

**If you add "ha" to Abram,
you get Abraham.**

Caution: Too Much Joking Can Kill

Genesis 19:14 (NCV):
So Lot went out and said to his future sons-in-law who were pledged to marry his daughters, "Hurry and leave this city! The Lord is about to destroy it!" But they thought Lot was joking.

And so the fiancés of his daughters die, 'cause they think Lot's just joking. Obviously, he joked with them before, or why else would they think that? Sadly, too much joking can be fatal. Humor heals; joking kills. I pray we have the wisdom to tell the difference. And if not, may we at least die laughing.

**What do you name your newborn son
when you're a century old?
... Laughter! (Isaac means laughter.)**

Isaac Would Love to Join Us, But He's All Tied Up

Genesis 22:6-9

Carrying the wood while Abraham carries the fire and the knife, insightful Isaac notices they have wood and fire, but no lamb for the burnt offering. "Uhhhh, Dad? Did you forget something? You know, like the lamb to be sacrificed?" Abraham tells his little tyke Ike that God will provide the lamb for the sacrifice. And fortunately for Isaac, God provided a ram to take his place in the fiery festivities. Although the Bible doesn't say, I'm sure, Abraham said these immortal words: "Don't tell your mother."

How Much Is That Tombsite in the Mountain?

Genesis 23

Sarah dies, so Abraham mourns and seeks a place to bury her. Out of sight. Out of scent! He talks to the Hittites and plays the Stranger/Sojourner Card. The Hittites think he's swell, so they tell him, "Take the best burial plot we've got!" Abraham bows and tells them to ask Ephron the son of Zohar to sell him the cave of Machpelah for its full price. But Ephron tells Abraham to take the cave as his gift. "In front of all my relatives, I give you the cave!" Abraham insists he will pay for the field. Ephron says the land is worth 400 shekels of silver and asks, "What is that between you and me?"

And so, Abraham pays that price. As if Ephron had said: "In front of my family and friends, I give you the field for free. For free! And you? You give me 400 shekels of silver. Also for free."

Esau Gets Stewed

Genesis 25:29-34
Esau sells his birthright for a bowl of lentil stew. No self-respect! At least hold out for Belgian waffles with strawberries and whipped cream. Or a Peanut Butter Chocolate Pie! Banana pudding with Vanilla wafers. Something tasty. But lentil stew? Hardly worth a birthright. You'd have to give me your birthright to get me to eat that. And possibly some Pepto-Bismol and Alka-Seltzer.

Jake the Snake Slithers Again

Genesis 27:43-45
Rebecca tells Jacob to stay with her brother Laban until Esau's anger subsides; and he forgets Jacob tricked him out of his birthright and blessing. Right. Like that's something easily forgotten.

Concrete Cushions
Do Not a Pillow Make

Genesis 28:11
Jacob uses a stone for a pillow. Some pillow! If he were wealthy, would his servant say?: "Would you like for me to fluff your rock, Sir?"

World's Worst First Date
(So Far Anyway)

Genesis 29:11
Jacob meets Rachel, kisses her, and weeps.
Kind of creepy and romantic at the same time.
Normally guys don't do that. Rachel must have
wondered if she needed a breath mint.

Divine Dreams,
The Way of Women,
And A Big Pile of Rocks

Genesis 31:22-55
Laban finds out that Jacob fled and pursues
him. But that night, God comes to Laban in a
dream and warns him not to speak to Jacob either
good or bad. And yet, the very next day, Laban
catches up to Jacob and yaps away. He even says
Jacob's God told him not to say anything to him.
Laban accuses Jacob of stealing his gods. Jacob has
the God who visited Laban in a dream, so why
would he need such silly trinkets as silent idols that
sit still, doing nothing? Unless he has a desk in a
drafty room and needs a paper weight. 'Cause other
than that, they're useless. Not knowing his beloved
Rachel stole the gods, he tells Laban to search
everywhere and kill whomever stole his idols. An
idol threat? The last place Laban checks is Rachel's
tent. She hid the so-called gods in a saddle upon
which she sits. She tells Laban not to be upset that

she can't rise to greet him, but "the way of women" is upon her. Hearing that, he probably cringed. So Laban can't find his idols. Jacob rants at Laban for all he suffered at his hand for the past twenty years. Laban rants back, reminding Jacob that all he has came from him. Laban suggests they build a mound of rocks as a witness between them, so they won't pass that pile of stones to harm each other. 'Cause nothing stops a fight from breaking out better than a big pile of rocks.

Sneaky Snaky Dan

Genesis 49:17 (ESV):
Dan shall be a serpent in the way,
a viper by the path, that bites the horse's heels
so that his rider falls backward.

You call that a blessing? I've heard better blessings from people I accidentally cut off in traffic.

EXODUS

Exodus could be called "Exit Us", because this is where God frees His chosen ones from Egypt. Joseph had saved Pharaoh and his folks from famine, but a new pharaoh came along and "He gypped" the Hebrews by enslaving them.

God uses Moses to free His people and gives us The Law through him. So you'd better do what "Mo Says".

Hello Lord,
Who Are You Again?

Exodus 3:13
Moses asks God His Name! "When the children of Israel ask me what Your name is, how should I answer them?" After 400 years of slavery in Egypt, the Hebrews forgot God's name! Poor Moses, it's so hard to ask the Name of Someone you know you're supposed to know.

How many times has this happened?: "And when I tell my folks I met the woman of my dreams, what should I say her name is again?" Slap! "Someone else!"

Here Am I!
Send ... Someone Else

Exodus 4: 1-17
Moses tries to weasel out of having to do God's will. Can anyone relate? He says no one's gonna believe him, so God tells him to throw his staff on the ground. He complies; and his staff turns into a snake. "Aaahhhh!!!!!!" Moses flees from it! God tells him to catch the snake by its tail; and after he does, it turns back into his staff. God makes Moses' hand leprous; and then heals it. God makes Moses turn water into blood. Even with God empowering him, Moses complains. "Me no talk so goodly." (A harsh paraphrase indeed.) He claims he's not eloquent, but slow of speech; and yet, every

time God asks him to do something, he fires back a
reason why he can't. God points out that He made
man's mouth; and that He will be with Moses'
vocal chords. But Moses pleads for Him to send
someone else. God saved his life as an infant in a
basket. Why else did God spare Moses' life if not
to lead His people to freedom? No other reason.
God invested 80 years into Moses' life; and He
wants to see some return on His investment!
Moses' brother Aaron visits, so God appoints him
to be Moses' spokesperson. And although Exodus
means way out, Moses has no way of getting out of
God's will.

You Must Be New to Rescuing;
You're Supposed to Make Things Better,
Not Worse!

Exodus 5:1-21

Moses and Aaron visit Pharaoh to tell him
the LORD says for him to let His people go, so they
can have a feast to Him in the wilderness. Pharaoh
asks, "Who is the LORD; and why should I obey
Him?" Moses explains, but Pharaoh claims Moses
prattles on about sacrifices in the wilderness
because the Hebrews are too idle. So he decides
they can supply their own straw, but still make the
same number of bricks. This gets the foremen
beaten. (Strikes me as a silly means of punishing a
worker. If you beat him, he'll be less likely to work
efficiently. So you're really hurting yourself.)

Thus, the people Moses tries to rescue get into deeper trouble and vent their anger at him and Aaron. They say in the ESV, "… you have made us stink in the sight of Pharaoh …" That's gotta be quite a stench, if you can see it!

**The Israelites fled from Pharaoh
after they caught him
running a pyramid scheme.**

By a Show of Hands,
How Many People
Hate to Raise Their Hands?

Exodus 17:8-13

The Amalekites fight the Israelites. And the way this battle works is whenever Moses holds up his hands, the Israelites prevail, but when he lowers them, the Amalekites prevail. So all the Israelites need to survive and become victorious is for Moses to keep his hands held high. But his hands get tired. Aaron and Hur sit Moses on a nice, comfy rock and hold up his hands for him until sunset, so Joshua and the Israelites defeat the Amalekites.

When Moses lowers his hands, Israelites die. This is a war of swords, so when one side prevails, the other side gets slaughtered. Or at the very least, stabbed in inconvenient places. Imagine Moses scratching his foot for a second or so. Suddenly he hears the screams of his kinfolk being sliced and diced. "Sorry! I had an itchy pinky toe!"

Loosen Your Necks;
And Fast!

Exodus 33:3 (NIV):
[God tells the Israelites]:
Go up to the land flowing with milk and honey.
But I will not go with you, because you are a stiff-
necked people and I might destroy you on the way.

Not a verse likely to be found on a Words of
Comfort greeting card.

Don't Blame Me;
Blame San Andreas;
It's His Fault!

Exodus 32:4 and 24
Aaron creates an idol of gold in the shape of
a calf. (Is this where we get the expression Holy
Cow?) When Moses asks him about it, Aaron says
he put the gold into the fire; and out came the calf.
Never once mentioning how he fashioned the gold
with a tool, he refuses to accept responsibility for
his own actions: "Don't blame me; blame the
flames!" It's like Adam and Eve all over again.
Without the slithering serpent and the itchy fig
leaves.

Although many have tried,
Moses is the only man in history
to break all Ten Commandments
at the same time.

If We Had More Fingers, Would We Have Gotten More Commandments?

Exodus 34:28 (ESV):
So he [Moses] was there with the LORD
forty days and forty nights.
He neither ate bread nor drank water.
And he wrote on the tablets
the words of the covenant,
the Ten Commandments.

See that? They're called the Ten Commandments, not the Ten Nifty Ideas.

Ten? Ten?! We couldn't handle having only one rule in the Garden of Eden, so what makes God think we can handle ten?

That's why I love my church so much. We chiseled the Ten Commandments down to Nine.

<u>LEVITICUS</u>

Leviticus has enough rules and regulations to make a "Levite Cuss". The name Leviticus means "Belonging to the Levites"; although some might argue that it means "Long-Winded".

Although Leviticus isn't a big laugh-getter, it's great for curing insomnia.

**Why can't I get a clean shave
without feeling like
I'm purifying the altar in Leviticus?**

For the Wicked:
Shaking Leaves Cause Quaking Knees

Leviticus 26:36 (NKJV):
'And as for those of you who are left, I will send
faintness into their hearts in the lands of their
enemies; the sound of a shaken leaf shall cause
them to flee; they shall flee as though fleeing from a
sword, and they shall fall when no one pursues.

Clumsy paranoiacs! Must be Magnolia
leaves blowing on the sidewalk; 'causes those are
loud and make me jump! But in a macho, dignified
manner.

NUMBERS

If Leviticus hadn't been boring enough,
Numbers lists genealogies galore. Thus, you could
say Leviticus makes you numb, but this book makes
you number. More than once.

Why Holy Men
Should Avoid Bad Hair Days

Numbers 6:1-21
Strict rules for those who vow to separate
themselves unto the LORD. If someone dies very
suddenly beside him, and he defiles his holy head of
hair, the former days will become null and void,
because his separation was defiled. Thus, when
someone dies suddenly next to the Nazirite, all the

time spent adhering to the strict regimen of a Nazirite is lost; and the Nazirite has to start all over.

I imagine some poor Nazirite who has dedicated himself for a year, but on the 365th day of his separation, some poor soul sitting next to him at dinner suddenly chokes to death on a chicken bone, so he has to start all over again. On the 365th day of the second year, someone else next to him has a fatal heart attack. Next year, a stray arrow takes out the person next to him. Next year, lightning. A falling anvil. Someone yodels causing an avalanche. Rabid porcupines attack. Etc. Thus, this poor Nazirite who planned to follow the strict regimen for just one year winds up spending the rest of his life trying to fulfill the demanding obligations and dies on the 365th day. Defiling the Nazirite next to him.

These Aren't My Kids!

Numbers 11:10-15

Moses hears the people crying, which angers the LORD; and doesn't make Moses all that happy either. So Moses asks God, "Why pick on me? Why make me responsible for all these cry babies? Did I spawn them that You make me baby-sit them? Why must I carry them to the land that You promised them? And where in this desolate wilderness am I supposed to find enough meat to feed these hungry folks? They keep weeping, sobbing all over me, pleading, 'Give us meat to eat!' These whiners are too much for me to bear.

If this is how You treat me, let me find favor in
Your sight; and zap me, so I don't suffer like this
anymore!"

Rarely found in prayer books: Moses'
famous "Zap Me, Zap Me Now" prayer. If being
killed is Moses' idea of finding favor, I'd hate to
hear what he considers disfavor.

Let's Try a Different Angle

Numbers 22, 23, and 24

Balak son of Zippor, king of Moab, sends
princes to hire Balaam son of Beor to curse the
Israelites. At first, Balaam tells him God won't let
him go to Balak. Instead of throwing money at a
problem, Balak throws princes. More numerous
and more noble! He sends the second best the first
time, but the second time he sends the first best.
Seems kind of backwards. But the man knows how
to negotiate: If you start at the tippy top, you have
nowhere to go, but down. He offers Baalam more
riches and honor than before. But Baalam tells the
princes to tell Balak that even if he offers his palace
full of silver and gold, Baalam cannot go beyond
what God tells him.

That night, God tells Baalam to go with the
men if they come to him, but instead, Baalam gets
up the next day and goes to them, so God sends His
armed angel with his sword drawn to block Baalam.
Baalam doesn't see the angel, but his donkey does,
so his donkey veers away from the avenging angel.
Three times! Veers off the path, smacks into a wall,

and with nowhere else to turn, the donkey plops down. Does Baalam thank his donkey for saving his life? No. He beats him three times with his staff! One for each rescue. And then God lets the animal speak for itself: Yes, Baalam's donkey talks! David Meece calls him "the original Mister Ed".

What I find funnier than his donkey talking is Baalam carrying on a conversation with his animal without incredulity. Instead of thinking, "Wow! This is amazing! My donkey can speak!" He just talks with it like it's no big deal. He even gripes: "You made a fool of me!" Sorry, Baalam. That wasn't the donkey's fault.

After Baalam and his donkey finish their heart-to-heart conversation, the LORD opens Baalam's eyes so he sees the angel too. The angel rebukes Baalam for mistreating his animal which saved his life three times. Baalam admits he sinned. The angel of the LORD lets Baalam go to Balak, but warns him to speak only what the LORD tells him to say. And after that, as far as I know, Balaam and his donkey were no longer on speaking terms.

Meanwhile, Balak meets Baalam and asks him why he didn't arrive sooner. Baalam replies, "I'm here now." He again explains how he can only say what God tells him to say. A concept which continuously eludes Balak's grasp.

Baalam tells Balak to build him seven altars and to sacrifice seven bulls and seven rams. He must have been hungry from the long trip. Baalam blesses Israel, which clearly upsets Balak. "What have you done to me? I brought you here to curse my enemies; and you blessed them!" Baalam reiterates he can only say what God says to say.

So Balak takes Baalam to a different place where they can see only a part of Israel, as if God would want to curse them from that angle. And again, Balak has to pay for another seven altars, seven bulls, and seven rams. (That's fourteen each, so far. Not counting the travel expenses for all those princes.) And what does Baalam do? He blesses Israel again. Befuddled beyond belief, Balak blurts out, "Neither curse them at all, nor bless them at all." Again, Baalam explains how he must say only what God tells him to say.

Does Balak realize God doesn't want to curse Israel? Baalam's told him that more than once. But no, Balak takes Baalam to another spot, thinking that new place will make God want to curse Israel. Which adds yet another seven altars, seven bulls, and seven rams to the tally. And does the new position persuade God to curse His people? Of course not. Baalam blesses them again. Balak blows his top. "I brought you here to curse my enemies; and you've blessed them three times! Go home! I would have paid you handsomely, but the LORD has held you back from making the big bucks!" Baalam reminds Balak that from the get-go, he told his messengers that even if Balak offered his palace full of silver and gold, Baalam could not go beyond what God tells him to say. Before leaving, Baalam bandies about more oracles, including Messianic prophecies of a Star coming out of Jacob and a Scepter arising from Israel.

Baalam and Balak part ways. Balak lost all that time plus the travel expenses for his princes to visit Baalam. Twice. Plus the costs of constructing twenty-one altars and sacrificing twenty-one bulls and twenty-one rams. What did he get for all he paid to curse Israel? He got them blessed three times and heard their future glory foretold.

Lesson Learned: When you hire people, listen to them when they tell you their limitations. Otherwise, include a clause allowing you to claim a full refund if not satisfied! Why let all those altars, bulls, and rams go to waste?

"Slow Down, You Move Too Fast; You Got to Make the Morning Last"*

Lines written by Paul Simon from Simon and Garfunkel's 1966 song: "The 59th Street Bridge Song (Feelin' Groovy)".

Numbers 31:1

God tells Moses that after the Israelites fight the Midianites, Moses will be gathered to his people. Which is a nice way of saying kick the bucket, buy the farm, croak.

As Moses gathers the people to fight against the Midianites, I imagine him encouraging them to take their time, not to rush. "Haste makes waste." "You can never plan too much." "Slow and easy does it every time."

Reiterating the Laws of God to the Israelites, Moses manages to survive through the rest of the book of Numbers, all the way until Deuteronomy 34:5. He repeats himself so much, because his life depends on it!

DEUTERONOMY

Deuteronomy means "Second Law". Moses reiterates the commandments of God, so you could say, Deuteronomy means "Here we go again!"

"One Shoe Off, One Shoe On. Deedle, Deedle, Dumpling My Son John."*

* From the nursery rhyme: "Deedle, Deedle, Dumpling".

Deuteronomy 25:5-12
If brothers live together; and one of them dies and leaves no son, the widow must marry one of her brothers-in-law; and he must "honeymoon" with her to raise up offspring in his dead brother's name. Thus, their firstborn son would be raised in the name of his dead uncle. But if the brother of the dead man refuses to do his duty in this way (maybe she nags; can't cook; snores; whatever), then the widow can rat out her unenthusiastic brother-in-law to the town honchos. After the city council confers with the man, if he still refuses to impregnate his dead brother's widow, the widow will remove that man's sandal, spit in his face, and say, "That's what happens to the man who refuses to raise offspring

for his brother." And henceforth, that man shall be known in Israel as "The Clan of the Man Who Had His Sandal Removed".

Although I'm sure he'll be called by other names too. Naughty Brother. Loveless Uncle. Captain One Shoe.

Plagues Aplenty!

Deuteronomy 28:58-68

Moses issues several warnings to obey everything written in the Book of the Law and respect the Holy and Awesome Name of God, or a plethora of plagues will come upon you. A slew of dreadful diseases, some imported from Egypt, long, lingering sicknesses, even illnesses not listed in the Bible, until you are destroyed. And those who survive that, will become scattered among the nations where you'll serve "gods" of wood and stone. Synthetic gods who won't do you any good. How can you expect anything good from a "god" who can be eaten by termites? You won't enjoy much rest either. Constantly living with danger and fear. In the morning, you'll wish it were evening; and in the evening, you'll wish it were morning. Terror will fill your heart and grip your soul. Your eggs will be runny; your smashed potatoes, lumpy. (Unless you like them that way.) Your shoes will become untied; and you'll trip in front of your crush. Someone else will nab the free prize from the box of your favorite sugary breakfast cereal. Etc. The Lord will send you back to Egypt, even though Moses said you would never go back there. If all that isn't bad enough, you will offer yourselves for sale as slaves, but no one will buy you!

Reminds me of a sketch on NBC's "Saturday Night Live" where Ringo Starr is being auctioned at a sale of Beatles' memorabilia. Ringo! The Beatles' drummer! At first, no one bids for him. No one! But then someone asks if the jacket Ringo's wearing might have been worn by Paul. The auctioneer says maybe. And then people start to bid.

JOSHUA

His name means "Yahweh Is Salvation"; and leading the children of Israel after Moses dies, Joshua has some really big sandals to fill.

Just as Disobedient?

Joshua 1:17a (ESV):
Just as we obeyed Moses in all things,
so we will obey you.

The people of Israel promise to be as obedient to Joshua as they had been to Moses. Well, that can't be good.

**Joshuopoloy is the exciting game
where you help the Israelites
conquer the Promised Land.
"I just rolled a seven, Jericho.
Your walls are tumbling down!"**

A Stale Performance Indeed,
But at Least They Passed the Audition

Joshua 9:1-26

Fearing for their lives, the Gibeonites pretend to travel from afar to make peace with the Israelites. They even use costuming and props, wearing tattered clothes and battered sandals and carrying worn-out sacks, old wineskins, and moldy bread! Forgetting to ask God's opinion, the Israelite leaders make a treaty with them. Their crummy acting pays off! Three days later, the Israelites uncover the Gibeonites' ruse. Joshua asks why they tricked them. Duh! To save their lives. No one likes to be slaughtered. The Gibeonites agree to become woodcutters and water carriers, which sounds tedious, but in the end, is way better than dying. Unless you drown in a vat of gooey fudge.

JUDGES

When Jesus said, "Judge not"; He didn't mean for us not to read this book.

Burn More Calories than You Eat;
Or Plug Into a Lipo Machine

Judges 3:12-30

This may come as a surprise, but even after the LORD rescued His people from Egypt, gave them the Promised Land, and saved them therein many times too, the Israelites sin again. So God gives them into the hands of Eglon, the hefty, plus-sized king of Moab who joins with the Ammonites and Amalekites to attack Israel and take over the City of Palms. (A.k.a. Jericho.) Which really wasn't that big a deal, seeing how the walls needed repair. But still. That upset the people of Israel, so they cried out to God.

So God gives them a left-handed man named Ehud. Being sent to take tribute to Eglon, Ehud fashions a double-edged dagger a cubit long. (About 18 inches. So it's either a Jumbo Dagger or a Mini-Sword. You choose.) And he puts this foot-and-a-half long Pointy Weapon on his right thigh, because back then, that's how left-handed people wore their Pointy Weapons.

The bouncers at the door of the King's Palace check Ehud's left thigh, and not finding any weapons attached, pointy or otherwise, let him crash the party. Once inside, he tells the king he has a secret message for him. Eglon hushes everyone else and kicks them out, so he can hear this clandestine communication. Once alone, Ehud thrusts his Sharp Stick of Steel into Eglon's stomach, even the handle sinks into his big belly; with Eglon's fat closing over his weapon, Ehud decides he can always fashion a new one, if need be. Not enough Lysol in the world would make that blade worth holding again.

Ehud locks the door behind himself and flees. And, since he no longer has a weapon attached to his right thigh, he runs quicker.

The king's servants return and find the door locked. They figure Eglon must be going to the bathroom, so they wait a little while. But eventually they think even a king his size should be done by now, so they search for a key, unlock the door, and find Eglon dead. Fortunately for Ehud, the "propriety" of Eglon's servants gave him time to slip away. He sounds a trumpet and calls an army together to defeat the Moabites.

The point is: Cut back on the Twinkies, exercise, and beware of Lefties with pointy right thighs who promise to share secret messages.

So Long Sisera

Judges 4-5

After Ehud dies, Israel runs rogue again, incurring the wrath of God. Some Chosen People just never learn! But God raises up a prophetess named Deborah to save them. She tells Barak to lead the Israelites against Sisera and the Canaanite army under his command. Barak says, "Okey-dokey, but only if you go with me." Deborah agrees, but since he made such an uncourageous request, she says the glory of defeating Sisera will be given to a woman, not him.

Barak's army proves victorious, so Sisera flees from battle and hides in the tent of Jael, a Kenite woman. She offers him milk to quench his thirst, lulls him to sleep, and pounds a tent peg through his temple. Abruptly ending his dreams, his life, and his career.

To celebrate the happy occasion (happy for the Israelites, not the Canaanites, and certainly not for Sisera), Deborah composes a song. Near the end, she sings about Sisera's mother gazing out her window and wondering why Sisera takes so long to return home. What delays the chatter of his chariots? But she and the women with her console themselves thinking the Canaanite soldiers must be dividing the plunder and doling out a girl, or two, for every man. Sounds like the Jan & Dean song: "Surf City" (written by Brian Wilson and Jan Berry) with the line: "Two girls for every boy."

The name Jael means mountain goat; and she used milk to lure Sisera to sleep. Goat milk?

I want to go quietly in my sleep. Like Sisera. Without the tent peg. And minus the goat milk. Unless it's chocolate. And it better be strong and tasty chocolate too.

Gideon's Bible
(Or At Least His Part Therein)

Judges 6-8

Gideon asks God for the sign of the fleece. He says if dew is on the fleece only; and the ground is dry, he'll know for sure God will save Israel by his hand, just as He said. God does so, but Gideon still isn't convinced, even though he said he would be. So Gideon asks for the opposite! Dry fleece, wet ground. Which God gives. Before that, Gideon asked the Angel who spoke to him for a sign too. The Angel complied by causing fire to rise from a rock and devour goat meat and unleavened bread.

That's three signs! Thomas isn't the only doubter in the Bible. For a fourth sign, God gets Gideon to eavesdrop at the enemy camp. Gideon hears two soldiers talking. One recounts his dream about a loaf of barley bread that tumbled into their camp, causing a tent to collapse. Ever the wise dream-interpreter, his buddy tells him the tumbling barley bread must be the sword of Gideon the son of Joash, a man of Israel, because God's going to give him the Midian army. How does one interpret tumbling barley bread so specifically?

Bad Boy Abimelech

Judges 9

The illegitimate son of a slave woman, Abimelech convinces the people of Shechem to let him rule over them, instead of Jerubbaal's seventy legitimate sons. Gotta love Abimelech's sales pitch: Never mind if I'm the best ruler; I'm your relative!

Upset at barely surviving the killing of his sixty-nine brothers, Jotham yells from a nearby mountaintop to tell "The Parable of the Trees": The trees want to choose a king to reign over them, so they approach the olive tree which refuses, being too busy producing olive oil. The fig tree's too busy growing its sweet fruit. And the grapevine's too busy wining. Red and white. But the thorn bush has nothing better to do, so it agrees to reign as King of the Trees, if the trees really want it to.

But if they don't, then fire should spring forth from the thorn bush to devour the cedars of Lebanon. (And if the cedars of Lebanon are such a big deal, why didn't the other trees make them king?)

Jotham's rousing rendition of "The King of Trees" proves to be an elegant way of saying, "Nyah nyah nyah nyah nyah! You're a bramble bush! You ain't nothin', but a bunch o' thorns!"

After that, he berates them eloquently, saying if they honored their hero Gideon by treating his seventy sons as they deserved, they should live happily ever after. But if not, (and they didn't, since they slaughtered sixty-nine of them), fire should come from Abimelech and from the people of Shechem and Beth-millo and devour each other.

Gaal the son of Ebed moves into Shechem, badmouths Abimelech, and gets the Shechemites to back him instead. Gaal boasts that if he were in charge, he'd remove Abimelech. Meanwhile Zebul, the ruler of the city, becomes angered at hearing Gaal's gaul. So he tells Abimelech to set an ambush against the city. Abimelech gathers his men; and in the early morning hours, they march toward the city. Gaal sees this and tells Zebul that men approach from the mountains. Zebul says Gaal's seeing things, that he's mistaking the shadows for soldiers. Gaal sees another troop coming from another direction. So Zebul breaks the bad news to him, that Abimelech has arrived to defeat him. Zebul asks Gaal, "Where is your mouth now?"

And then, this chapter ends with a woman

atop a tower in Thebez dropping a millstone on Abimelech's head. Barely alive, he pleads with his armor bearer to slay him with a sword, so people won't say a woman killed him. (Which they do anyway in 2 Samuel 11:21.) The son of a slave woman and the murderer of 69 out of 70 of his half-brothers, Abimelech's life ends as a chauvinist with a cracked skull. Pop goes the weasel!

Lesson Learned: Treat women with respect. And don't let them get you stoned.

Son of a Naughty Girl
a.k.a. Jephthah Hookerson

From Judges 11 (RSV):

Verse 1: "Now Jephthah the Gileadite was a mighty warrior, but he was the son of a harlot. Gilead was the father of Jephthah."

Verses 7-8: "But Jephthah said to the elders of Gilead, "Did you not hate me, and drive me out of my father's house? Why have you come to me now when you are in trouble?" And the elders of Gilead said to Jephthah, "That is why we have turned to you now, that you may go with us and fight with the Ammonites, and be our head over all the inhabitants of Gilead.""

In other words, the elders of Gilead sayeth unto Jephthath: "Duh!"

30-31: "And Jephthah made a vow to the Lord, and said, 'If thou wilt give the Ammonites into my hand, then whoever comes forth from the doors of my house to meet me, when I return victorious from the Ammonites, shall be the Lord's, and I will offer him up for a burnt offering.'"

What a strange vow! What did Jephthah think would come out of the doors of his house to greet him? A sacrificial lamb? A bull without blemish? That annoying neighbor who makes weird noises at night?!

And with all those animals running around, what did his house smell like? This was way before Air Wick® and Febreze®.

34-35: "Then Jephthah came to his home at Mizpah; and behold, his daughter came out to meet him with timbrels and with dances; she was his only child; besides her he had neither son nor daughter. And when he saw her, he rent his clothes, and said, 'Alas, my daughter! you have brought me very low, and you have become the cause of great trouble to me; for I have opened my mouth to the Lord, and I cannot take back my vow.'"

He made the strange vow; and yet he's upset with her?! "Oh, Daddy. So sorry to inconvenience you. Excuse me for rushing out the door to welcome you home. Next time you make such a crazy vow, send a messenger ahead of you, so we can shove our noisy neighbor Abner out the door."

I'll Bet You Can't Say This!

Judges 12:5-6 (NCV):
The men of Gilead
captured the crossings of the Jordan River
that led to the country of Ephraim.

A person from Ephraim trying to escape would say,
"Let me cross the river."
Then the men of Gilead would ask him,
"Are you from Ephraim?" If he replied no,
they would say to him, "Say the word 'Shibboleth.'"
The men of Ephraim
could not say that word correctly.
So if the person from Ephraim said, "Sibboleth,"
the men of Gilead would kill him at the crossing.
So forty-two thousand people from Ephraim
were killed at that time.

When did mispronunciation become a capital offense? Forty-two thousand lives could've been saved, if only they had heard of Hooked on Phonics.

The Original Superman!
Did Samson Wear an "S" on His Belt?

Judges Chapters 13-17
Besides his great strength, Samson had a bit of a wit and a flair for poetics. Like Muhammad Ali with his "float like a butterfly and sting like a bee".
Samson's Riddle in Judges 14:14 (NASB): "Out of the eater came something to eat, And out of the strong came something sweet." An unsolvable riddle, unless you knew the carcass of a lion Samson killed housed a bunch of bees and their honey.
After the Philistines coerced his wife into making him reveal the answer, Samson derides

them in Judges 14:18 (NASB): "If you had not plowed with my heifer, You would not have found out my riddle." He calls his wife a heifer and then wonders why his father-in-law thinks he doesn't like her.

And what about Delilah? In Judges 16:1-22, Delilah pesters Samson for the secret of his strength. As soon as Samson tells her something, she tries it to no avail. Thus, she's trying to use whatever he says to destroy him. In verse 15 (NKJV), she has the gall to say: "How can you say, 'I love you,' when your heart is not with me? You have mocked me these three times and have not told me where your great strength lies." Crazy thing is, he finally tells her! Who would've thought a haircut could be a hero's "Kryptonite"?

What kind of suitcase
robs Samson of his powers?
... Samsonite.

For Micah

Judges 18
The children of Dan take away Micah's priest, idols, and ephod, so Micah gathers his neighbors together to pursue them. When Micah's group catches up to them, they say (RSV): "What ails you that you come with such a company?" Micah replies (RSV): "You take my gods which I made, and the priest, and go away, and what have I left? How then do you ask me, 'What ails you?'"

RUTH

The babe Ruth's name means "friendship". So in her memory; and in honor of friendship, eat a bunch of Baby Ruth bars. Or better yet, share some nutty chocolate with a friend! ... Hello, friend!

**One of two Moabite women
followed her mother-in-law back to Israel,
but the other one stomped home ruthlessly.**

Don't Call Me That!

Ruth 1:20-21 (NIV):
"Don't call me Naomi*," she told them.
"Call me Mara**, because the Almighty
has made my life very bitter. I went away full,
but the LORD has brought me back empty.
Why call me Naomi? The LORD has afflicted me;
the Almighty has brought misfortune upon me."

* Naomi means pleasant.
** Mara means bitter.

Naomi feels she's been misnamed. Like the way they call dinky candy bars "Fun Size", when the Super Mega-Deluxe Size is a lot more fun.

1 SAMUEL

Samuel means "Heard by God". Had Sam been a cow, his name would have meant herded.

What Have You Been Drinking?

1 Samuel 1:9-16

Hannah prays quietly, but moves her lips, which makes Eli the priest think she's drunk. Silly Eli. The silent moving of one's lips doesn't indicate drunkenness. Most drunks are far from silent. Many shout. Some yodel. Others "sing" karaoke.

This Is Why You Shouldn't Lean Back in Your Chairs, Kids

1 Samuel 4:18a (NIV):
When he [a man bringing news] mentioned the ark of God, Eli fell backward off his chair by the side of the gate. His neck was broken and he died,

When my friend Joel Dittmer taught school, he used that verse to discourage students from leaning back in their chairs.

Nothing a Little Preparation H Can't Cure

1 Samuel 5-6

After the Philistines capture the Ark of the Covenant, they become overrun with rats and tumors. Some scholars say that the word translated here as tumor means hemorrhoid. Which gives a whole new meaning to 1 Samuel 5:12: "the men who did not die were stricken with hemorrhoids, and the cry of the city went up to heaven."

When they returned the Ark, they included a chest with five golden rats and five golden tumors, a.k.a. five golden hemorrhoids. Can you imagine the look on the sculptor's face? "You want me to fashion five golden what?!"

This Year's Hide & Seek Champion

1 Samuel 10:22

Saul who has been chosen to be the first king of Israel hides among the equipment, the baggage.

When You Face Big Problems, Believe Bigger

1 Samuel 17:33 (NASB):
Then Saul said to David,
"You are not able to go against this Philistine
to fight with him; for you are but a youth
while he has been a warrior from his youth."

Goliath put the G in Giant! Which scared everyone except David. What Saul and the others failed to comprehend, is that David didn't let circumstances determine his demeanor. With his strong faith in God, David wasn't about to let a little thing like a giant ruin his day.

**The bigger they are,
the harder
… it is for them to hide!**

One Size Doesn't Fit All

1 Samuel 17:38-39

Saul who stands head and shoulders above everyone else in the land puts his armor on young David; and David tries to walk. In other words, the armor must have been several sizes too big, so instead of providing the protection he needs, the armor hampers his movement. Plus, a child wearing an adult's clothes is usually good for a chuckle.

**Killing Goliath with a stone
made David a rock star.**

"Stop Playing That Song!"*

* Variation of a line by Humphrey Bogart from the 1942 movie "Casablanca".

1 Samuel 18:7

The women seek to honor David, singing: "Saul has slain his thousands; and David, his ten thousands."

But their attempt to honor him endangers his life! First, with Saul. And later, with the Philistines when he flees to them to escape Saul. And this became sort of a deadly "running gag" coming back to haunt David at least two more times in 1 Samuel 21:11 and 29:5.

I wonder if David cried out to those women: "Stop honoring me! I want to live!"

David Can't Go to School Today

1 Samuel 19:11-16

When Saul seeks to kill David, David's wife Michal takes an image, covers it with goats' hair, and puts it in David's bed. When messengers come from Saul, she says David's sick in bed. How many times have you seen that trick pulled? Especially in "The Little Rascals" TV show from the 1950s and the 1996 movie "Ferris Bueller's Day Off".

There's No Shortage of Psychos in This Place

1 Samuel 21:10-15

To hide from Saul, David stays with Israel's enemies the Philistines. Hearing the Philistines talk about what a hero he is for the Israelites, David feigns madness, dribbling saliva down his beard and scratching the doorposts. Achish says in verse 15a (RSV): "Do I lack madmen, that you have brought this fellow to play the madman in my presence?"

Sayonara Samuel

1 Samuel 25:1

Samuel dies! There's still the rest of this chapter, chapters 26-31, and the entire book of 2 Samuel which bear his name; and he's dead. Why are these two books named after someone who doesn't make it through the first book, much less show up in the sequel?

The Labeling Theory in Action

1 Samuel 25:25

Nabal's name means Fool; and guess what? He acts foolish. What else would you expect? And who names their kid that in the first place?

So of course Bozo became a clown. With a name like that, what choice did he have?

You never hear this phrase: "The honorable Judge Bozo presiding." Or "You'll have to wait. Doctor Bozo is still in surgery."

2 SAMUEL

Samuel still means "Heard by God". The herd joke wasn't funny the first time, so I won't repeat it here. Although my timing may have been off before. Every show's different. Had he been a cow, ... Never mind. I see no reason to mention Sam again, since he doesn't show up this time around. And unlike Obi Wan Kenobi, not even his ghost appears! Not in Sammy 2.

Sword-Wielding
Is a Cutthroat Business!

2 Samuel 2:12-16

The men of Abner who served Ishbosheth the son of Saul and the men of Joab who fought for David meet and sit on opposite sides of the pool of Gibeon. Abner suggests to Joab that their men compete before them. Joab agrees. Twelve soldiers from each army, arise, grab their opponents, thrust them through with their swords, and they all fall down. Dead. Both sides kill each other! Someone nifty names that place "Helkath-hazzurim". But that name doesn't catch on, until someone says Helkath-hazzurim means the Field of Sharp Swords, Field of Daggers, or the Field of Hostilities. A.k.a. The Field of Sharp Pointy Things.

Hungry Swords

2 Samuel 2:26

Fleeing for his life, Abner calls out to Joab, "Shall the sword devour forever?" And then he explains how the end will be bitter and asks how long it will be before he tells his people to stop pursuing their brothers.

Abner started this fight; and yet he complains about it! Probably because his side lost. 360-19 according to 2 Samuel 2:30-31. And after 12 from each side dropped down in the Stab-A-Thon, that means his side lost 348-7. Don't start fights, if you can't fight. I mean: Don't start fights at all. But especially, if you can't fight. Like that fight-starting bully in the YouTube video who got beat up.

Yes, But as Far as Dead Dogs Go, He's One of the Best

2 Samuel 9:8 (NKJV):
Then he [Mephibosheth] bowed himself, and said,

"What is your servant,
that you should look upon such a dead dog as I?"

Talk about a poor self-image. Sounds like someone could use a hug!

"Come On Baby, Light My Fire"*

* *From The Doors' 1967 song "Light My Fire".*

2 Samuel 14:29-31 (NIV)
Then Absalom sent for Joab
in order to send him to the king,
but Joab refused to come to him. So he sent a
second time,
but he refused to come.
Then he said to his servants,
"Look, Joab's field is next to mine,
and he has barley there. Go and set it on fire."
So Absalom's servants set the field on fire.
Then Joab did go to Absalom's house
and he said to him,
"Why have your servants set my field on fire?"

Why? 'Cause that was the only way he knew to get a response out of Joab.

And it worked! So when subtlety fails, try being less subtle.

Although that's a hot idea for gaining someone's attention, both Smokey the Bear and I do not recommend resorting to pyrotechnics. Instead, try skywriting. Or a candy gram. A chocolate candy gram.

So and So Was My Idea!

2 Samuel 17:15 (NIV):
Hushai told Zadok and Abiathar,
"Ahithophel has advised Absalom such and such,
but I have advised to do so and so."

So and so beats such and such every time!

Ahithophel Finally Gets the Hang of It

2 Samuel 17:23
When his advice isn't followed, Ahithophel goes home, puts his house in order, and hangs himself. Apparently, he doesn't handle rejection well. He'd never have made it as an author or actor. Or even a salesperson. Especially the guy still selling VCRs.

Another Fine Product from Monuments R Us

2 Samuel 18:18
Absalom, like Saul, built himself a monument. Indeed, pride goes before a fall. And so does summer.

Is Spring Water Out of Date in Winter?

2 Samuel 23:14-17
During yet another fight with the Philistines,

David mentions how much he longs for a drink of water from the well in Bethlehem. To keep the king content, his top three mighty men battle through enemy lines to fetch him a cup of water from that well. The image of soldiers fighting with swords and clubs while trying to prevent a cup of water from spilling strikes me as slapsticky. Definitely not dry humor. But when they bring the wa-wa back to David, he pours it out, saying he can't drink it, because it's "the blood" of the men who risked their lives to fetch it for him. So they risked their lives for nothing! David didn't even drink it.

I have never understood his reasoning here. I think he should have savored every drop. To me, pouring it out showed how little he thought of the risk they took for him, instead of the opposite that he tried to convey. Like someone saying "Let's be friends." means: "Let's be strangers." And "Maybe some other time." means: "Not in a million years!"

1 KINGS

Kings means more than one king.

"1 Kings" looks like an oxymoron. If there's only one king, why is "1 Kings" plural?

You Can't Kill Me, 'Cause I'm Hiding in the Sacred Room Where They Slaughter Animals ... Oh-Oh!

1 Kings 1:41-53

After Adonijah made himself king without

his father's permission, he and those with him hear an uproar. Jonathan, a messenger, arrives; and Adonijah says: "Come in, for you are a prominent man, and bring good news." Jonathan replies, "No! Our lord King David has made Solomon king." Fearing Solomon will kill him, Adonijah flees to the altar and clutches its horns, figuring Solomon won't slay him before the altar of God. Even though that's the place for slaughtering sacrificial animals. How could he possibly think he'd be safe in The Slaughter Room? That room's built for bloodshed!

Famous Last Words

1 Kings 2:6 (NKJV):
[David said to Solomon,]
"Therefore do according to your wisdom,
and do not let his gray hair
go down to the grave in peace."

That's a nice way of saying, "You're a smart kid, figure out how to kill him in a way that makes me look good."

King David had sworn to Shimei that he wouldn't have him executed for his insolence. Since oaths only last until the death of the oath-maker, David's in the clear, because he'll be dead before Solomon executes Shimei. When it comes to taking oaths, that's quite a sneaky loophole!

Oaths expiring upon death must be why most zombies never marry. That; and it's so hard to find a caterer who serves brains.

Israel Idol

1 Kings (Overview)

Strikes me as odd, yet somewhat humorous, that the kings who destroy the kings before them for having idols continue to have the same idols!

I Promise I'll Do Whatever You Want, Unless You Want Me to Do Something I Don't Want to Do

1 Kings 2:13-23

With the help of Joab and several other key officials, Adonijah declared himself king. The people cried out, "Long live King Adonijah!" But Nathan got wind of the matter, even though his invitation "got lost in the mail". So he convinced Bathsheba to remind King David that he promised to make Solomon king. So David did. Solomon promised Adonijah that if he proved worthy, he'd be allowed to live. So now in these verses …

Adonijah approaches Bathsheba. He has only one request. He wants to marry Abishag the Shunammite, the beautiful virgin the people of Israel found to keep King David warm at night. That's all she did, so her maidenhood remained intact. Adonijah has the hots for her and asks Bathsheba to get Solomon to give her to him as his wife. She tells her son, the king, not to refuse her small request. Solomon replies that he will not refuse her. She tells him to let Adonijah marry Abishag the Shunammite. Solomon's reply?

He orders Adonijah executed.

"Whatever you want. I will not refuse you."
… "No way!" Talk about a quick 180-degree turn!
And poor Adonijah. He loses his throne, never gets
to honeymoon with the hottest virgin around, and
dies from Beheaded Syndrome.

Bathroom Humor
of Biblical Proportions

1 Kings 18:27 (NKJV):
And so it was, at noon,
that Elijah mocked them [the prophets of Baal]
and said, "Cry aloud, for he [Baal] is a god;
either he is meditating, or he is busy,
or he is on a journey,
or perhaps he is sleeping and must be awakened."

Elijah mocks the prophets of Baal because
they have received no response from their false god.
"Is busy" is a nice way of saying going to the
restroom. The NLT says: "relieving himself"*.

* Scripture quotation taken from the Holy Bible,
New Living Translation, copyright © 1996. Used by
permission of Tyndale House Publishers, Inc.,
Wheaton, Illinois 60189. All rights reserved.

Purina Lion Chow

1 Kings 20:35-43
A prophet tells a man to hit him, but he
doesn't want to strike a prophet, so for not obeying,

he gets killed by a lion. A no-win situation for that
guy. Not wanting to feed the wildlife, the second
guy punches the man of God. And with his
pulsating bruise, the prophet pretends to be a man
from battle to accuse Ahab. Similar to Nathan's
"You are the man!" Only this prophet's less of a
storyteller, and more of a method actor.

2 KINGS

Kings still means more than one king.
Especially 2 Kings.

Always Respect Chrome Domes

2 Kings 2:23-24 (NASB):
Then he [Elisha] went up from there to Bethel;
and as he was going up by the way,
young lads came out from the city
and mocked him and said to him,
"Go up, you baldhead; go up, you baldhead!"
When he looked behind him and saw them,
he cursed them in the name of the LORD.
Then two female bears came out of the woods
and tore up forty-two lads of their number.

Having wild animals kill kids for calling you
names is quite a far cry from Jesus' "Father forgive
them, for they know not what they do." And while
that sounds reprehensible for a prophet of God to
call a couple Momma Bears to maul 42 boys
because he doesn't like being labeled "Follicularly-
Challenged", I read where the "young lads" weren't

little boys, but a gang of teen terrorists that endangered him. Their cry of "Go up" was in reference to Elijah having ascended to Heaven. Thus, much more than mere mocking, they threatened Elisha's life.

So then, not only to avoid being mauled by she bears, but also to be loving and kind, let's be respectful and sensitive to the Kojak's, Daddy Warbucks', and Elmer Fudd's who "no longer need combs" and encourage Cue Balls and Shiny Heads alike by reassuring them as shown on the USA Network's super TV show "Psych", when Shawn Spencer's girlfriend Abigail told his bald daddy: "You're not bald, you're just taller than your hair."

Once Upon a Time There Was This Thistle

2 Kings 14:8-14

After defeating Edom, Amaziah king of Judah sends word to Jehoash king of Israel that they should engage in battle. Jehoash replies with this thistle story: The thistle in Lebanon asks a cedar to give his daughter to the thistle's son for a wife. But a wild beast passing by, steps on the thistle. Thus crushing the thistle's wedding plans. Jehoash warns Amaziah to stay at home and be content with his victory against Edom. Amaziah refuses. Jehoash defeats him and plunders the temple!

So apparently, the word amazing doesn't come from Amaziah. For he was deeply smitten. But not in a good way.

Don't Wake Up Dead

2 Kings 19:35b (KJV):
… and when they arose early in the morning,
behold, they were all dead corpses.

When they awoke, they were dead. What?!
Talk about a tough mourning.

1 CHRONICLES

Chronicles is just as exciting as the name implies. Or not. Almost as numbing as Numbers.

You Call This Praise?!

1 Chronicles 29:14 (NIV):
"We are aliens and strangers in your sight,
as were all our forefathers.
Our days on earth are like a shadow,
without hope."

In the midst of praising God, King David prays this verse that I find far from complimentary. Surely the sweet Psalmist of Israel should know what praise means. Yet another verse not to be found on a Words of Comfort greeting card.

2 CHRONICLES

2 Chronicles is a little less somniferous than 1 Chronicles. Less counting, or rather, recounting; and more action. But still, for the most part, this is

the re-telling of tales from 1 and 2 Kings, so you must struggle to overcome the overwhelming sensation of déjà vu.

"That's the Way You Do It: Get Your Money for Nothing"*

* From the 1981 Dire Straits' song "Money for Nothing" written by Mark Knopfler and Sting.

2 Chronicles 25:6-10

King Amaziah hires soldiers from Israel to help Judah fight against the men of Seir. He pays a thousand talents of silver for 100,000 soldiers! That's 100 for every talent. But a man of God tells Amaziah that he can't let the Israelites fight with his army, for the Lord is not with Israel. Amaziah inquires about the money he already spent. The man of God tells him that God is able to give him much more than that. So he sends the Israelite army away; and they leave in a rage. But why? They got paid a thousand talents to do nothing! They should be happy! They should party like it's 796 BC.

Idol-Worshippers Wonder Why God's Prophets Always Prophesy Evil Tidings for Them

2 Chronicles 25:14-16

Amaziah defeats the Edomites. Defeats them. His army wins! What does he do next? He brings back the idols of the people he defeated and burns incense to them! Naturally, this angers God. So he sends a prophet to ask Amaziah why he would seek so-called gods which couldn't rescue their people from his own attack. In other words: Why mess with loser idols? Amaziah arrogantly asks who made the prophet the king's advisor, tells him to stop talking, and asks why should he make him kill him. Probably having tasted chocolate at some point in his life, the prophet's not eager to die, so he issues one last warning and leaves.

EZRA

Ezra means "Help"; and that is what Ezra needs to build the temple. He's a priest, so he wants the temple rebuilt to give himself job security. Ezra doesn't even show up until chapter 7, but he has such a good agent and such a great P. R. team, that he still gets the book named after himself.

And We'll Have Funds, Funds, Funds, Till Daddy Takes Our T-Bills Away!*

My spoof of the 1964 Beach Boys' song "Fun, Fun, Fun" written by Brian Wilson and Mike Love.

Ezra

Cyrus king of Persia commands the people of God to rebuild the temple in Jerusalem. Fiendish folks from beyond the Euphrates River try to thwart the people of Judah and Benjamin and the Levites who attempt to reconstruct the house of God. So the bad guys write a letter to King Darius, tattling on the good guys for rebuilding the temple, saying the city of Jerusalem has a long history of sedition, and claiming that once Zion gets an Extreme City Makeover, her people will revolt, which will cause the king to lose all their taxes and revenue. Surely, such a letter will cease the reconstruction project. But King Darius checks the royal archives and discovers King Cyrus decreed the work be done, so Darius writes back and tells the bad guys to collect money from themselves to provide the resources needed to help rebuild the temple. So they went from trying to stop the project to having to fund it!

NEHEMIAH

Ezra 2: The Sequel! Nehemiah means "Yahweh Is Comfort"; and although considered authored by Nehemiah, this book figures as a sequel of sorts to Ezra. After the temple gets rebuilt, the next logical step is to rebuild the city walls. Ezra, temple; Nehemiah, walls. Got it?

Royal Bummer!

Nehemiah 2:1-8
Nehemiah, the cupbearer for King Artaxerxes, hears of the horrid state of Jerusalem and, for the first time, displays sadness before the king. Obviously, when you have someone drink your wine to make sure it's not poisoned, you'll be highly concerned about how they feel. Realizing

Nehemiah's neither sick nor poisoned, he determines he's just sad. After Nehemiah explains how upset he feels that Jerusalem lies in burned ruins with her walls broken down, the king gives him permission to go and rebuild the city. And why not? Who wants a cupbearer who's gonna mope around the place? Why let his droopy mood drag everyone else down?

Foxy Wallbanger

Nehemiah 4:3 (NKJV):
Now Tobiah the Ammonite was beside him,
and he said, "Whatever they build,
if even a fox goes up on it,
he will break down their stone wall."

That's probably the funniest thing Tobiah ever said. Which must be why he's so evil. He has no sense of humor. He thinks he does, but doesn't. Which is the worst kind of unfunny person. After he made his fox "joke", I wonder how long he chuckled before he realized he was the only one doing so.

Fibber McGee!

Nehemiah 6:8 (NIV):
I [Nehemiah] sent him [Sanballat] this reply:
"Nothing like what you are saying is happening;
you are just making it up out of your head."

That's the ancient way of saying "You're out of your mind!" or "You so crazy!"

<u>ESTHER</u>

Esther means "Star". She shines so bright, she wins a Beauty Contest! The kind of blessed babe for which every holy hunk prays. Preys?

Okay, If You Insist

Esther 1:15-21

Having removed Vashti from being queen because she refused to respond to his summons, King Xerxes finds himself wifeless. His personal servants suggest beautiful young virgins be sought for the king. He should appoint officers to bring the best hotties into his harem. And then, from a whole slew of bathing beauties, the king can pick someone to take Vashti's place. As the KJV puts it: "And the thing pleased the king; and he did so." Like Mel Brooks said in his 1981 movie "History of the World Part 1": "It's good to be the king!"

A Holy Hottie for the Lord

Esther

The book of Esther is like a textbook on how to write a great comedy. Make a villain pompous and evil like Haman. And give him a righteous rival like Mordecai. Haman resents the fact that Mordecai won't offer him homage. His prestige seems meaningless to himself, because Mordecai refuses to acknowledge his status. (Pride is often the "fatal flaw". The deflation of pomposity is a key element in many forms of humor.)

Haman seeks to destroy not just Mordecai, but his people, the Jews. And although He's not mentioned in this book, God has other plans.

Haman's Humiliation

Esther 6:4-12

Haman visits the king to ask permission to hang Mordecai on the seventy-five-feet high gallows he built for him. But before he can say anything, the king asks, "What should be done for the one the king wants to honor?" Using his astounding powers of arrogance, Haman thinks he's the only one the king would want to honor, so he tells him to have the one he wants to honor wear one of the king's robes and ride a royal horse, while a noble prince parades him through the city square and proclaims: "This is how we treat the one the king wants to honor!" The king likes the idea and tells Haman to do so for Mordecai. Humiliated, Haman parades his nemesis through the city square and proclaims: "This is how we treat the one the king wants to honor!" Afterwards, Haman covers his head and weeps-weeps-weeps all the way home.

The Pawn Fails to Take the Queen

Esther 6:14-7:8

Haman's only comfort is being the only one besides the king who's invited to a private meal prepared by queen Esther. At the banquet, however,

Esther exposes Haman as the evil villain who seeks to destroy her people. The king leaves in a rage to consider what to do. Haman pleads for his life, but in doing so, he falls across the couch where Esther is. That's when the king returns and says, "Will he also assault the queen while I am in the house?"

Hasta La Vista Haman!

Esther 7:10a (NKJV):
So they hanged Haman on the gallows
that he had prepared for Mordecai.

Perfect Ending: The villain gets caught in his own trap. Kind of like Wiley Coyote.

JOB

Meaning unknown? Sounds like a copout! Just because they don't know the meaning doesn't mean the meaning's unknown. It's just not known to them. A second source said that the name Job means "Persecuted, Oppressed". Ew! I'd rather think the meaning was unknown than to think his parents named him that!

The Movie Trailer for Job: "One man caught in a game between the forces of good and evil. His patience will be tested. His faith will be tried. His wife will be nagging. His comforting friends will offer no comfort at all. But if he remains true to the end, he'll double his profits and wind up with his own book in the Bible. So good job, Job!"

If You Remain Silent,
You Won't Say Anything Stupid!

Job 13:5 (RSV):
"Oh that you would keep silent,
and it would be your wisdom!"

Like the 1979 movie "Being There" where people think Peter Sellers' simpleton character is a genius, simply because he doesn't say much.

I like how the NCV phrases that verse too:

"I wish you would just stop talking;
then you would really be wise!"

You're as Comforting
as Concrete Cushions

Job 16:2 (RSV):
"I have heard many such things;
miserable comforters are you all."

Or today, he might say, "I've gotten better consolation from politicians."

Wise Men Wanted

Job 17:10 (NIV):
"But come on, all of you, try again!
I will not find a wise man among you."

Which means they can't put on a Christmas play, 'cause you need at least three.

What an <u>Udder</u> Disgrace!

Job 18:2-3 (NIV):
"When will you end these speeches?
Be sensible, and then we can talk.
Why are we regarded as cattle
and considered stupid in your sight?"

Could be your mooing. Or the brand on your back side; the way you herd together; or how much fun country folks have tipping you over.

Mock On! You Mock and Molars!

Job 21:3 (RSV):
"Bear with me, and I will speak,
and after I have spoken, mock on."

Sounds like Job's saying: Take a break from mocking me for a moment, so I can say something; and then, by all means, resume ridiculing. Scorn, scoff, deride! Disparage and disdain if you must. Sneer and jeer. Revile a while. Belittle a little. But wait at least thirty minutes after eating; or you might get cramps.

The Answer for All Your True-False Questions Is False

Job 21:34 (NIV):
"So how can you console me with your nonsense?
Nothing is left of your answers but falsehood!"

What an easy test!   Answer F for every question.   Do that with any True-False test; and more than likely, that's what you'll get. An F.

The Naked Truth about Nakedness

Job 24:7 (NKJV):
"They spend the night naked, without clothing,
And have no covering in the cold."

Yep, without clothing and having no covering is what naked means.

Kids Today Have No Respect

Job 30:1 (NIV):
"But now they mock me, men younger than I,
whose fathers I would have disdained
to put with my sheep dogs."

And those sheep dogs are extremely grateful.

God Is The Creator;
And We, the Createes

Job 38:1-11 et. al.
God appears to Job and tells him that God is God; and we are not. Especially Job. Like the way Chevy Chase would say on "Saturday Night Live": "I'm Chevy Chase; and you're not." Job 38:2 is not a compliment: "Who is this who darkens counsel with words without knowledge?" In Job 38:4-5a, God jests with Job, suggesting that he must know

how God created the Earth and such: "Where were you when I laid the foundations of the earth? Tell Me, if you understand. Who determined its dimensions? Surely you know!" Shirley might know, but Job sure doesn't.

Wisdom-Challenged

Job 39:13-18 (NCV):
"The wings of the ostrich flap happily,
but they are not like the feathers of the stork.
The ostrich lays its eggs on the ground
and lets them warm in the sand.
It does not stop to think that a foot might
step on them and crush them; it does not care
that some animal might walk on them.
The ostrich is cruel to its young,
as if they were not even its own.
It does not care that its work is for nothing,
because God did not give the ostrich wisdom;
God did not give it a share of good sense.
But when the ostrich gets up to run,
it is so fast that it laughs at the horse and its rider."

What better way for one who lacks wisdom to survive, than to run fast! I run fast. Never mind.

<u>PSALMS</u>

Psalms means "Praises". This book doesn't have chapters! Psalms contains 150 psalms. So you say, "Psalm 23", not "Psalms chapter 23".

Unless you want to appear foolish. Like pronouncing Job "job".

See La!

The Book of Psalms
The word Selah is defined in the footnote of the NIV as "A word of uncertain meaning occurring frequently in Psalms; possibly a musical term."
A musical term? That could mean anything from play softly to make it funky now! Hoo! Hoo!

Boy, You've Got Some Explaining to Do!

Psalm 7:14 (NIV):
He who is pregnant with evil
and conceives trouble gives birth to disillusionment.

"He who is pregnant ... gives birth": The man in labor gag, always a classic.

Shepherd Wanted?

Psalm 23:1 (KJV)
The LORD is my shepherd; I shall not want.

As Paul says in 1 Corinthians 13:11, when I was a child, I thought like a child, I reasoned as a child, etc. I used to read this and wonder what was wrong with the LORD being our shepherd that King David said we shall not want Him?
Oh, right. Like I was the only one who ever thought that.

Don't Be Intense

Psalm 84:10b (RSV):
I would rather be a doorkeeper
in the house of my God
than dwell in the tents of wickedness.

Duh! The house of God's air-conditioned.
And the hot tents of wickedness have mosquitoes.

What to Say
to a Man Wearing Short Shorts

Psalm 147:10b (NKJV):
He [The LORD] takes no pleasure
in the legs of a man.

Neither do I. In this way, I truly am divine.

<u>PROVERBS</u>

The gist of Proverbs? Yay wisdom; boo foolishness. The word proverb comes from the Latin *pro* meaning forth and *verbum* meaning word. Thus, *proverbum* means forth word. Which seems awfully forward. And if that does mean foreword, why isn't Proverbs before Genesis?

Solomon had a lot to say about Lazy Boys. He also waxed eloquently about Women, especially Naughty Gals and Contentious Drips. If we tackle the ladies first, that'll give the lazies longer to nap.

Sol's Gals

Proverbs says plenty about gals, especially wicked ones in chapters 5-7, but these are the best:

Drip, Drip, Drip

Proverbs 27:15-16 (NIV):
A quarrelsome wife is like a constant dripping
on a rainy day; restraining her is like
restraining the wind or grasping oil with the hand.

Like Patrick Swayze sang in the 1987 movie "Dirty Dancing": "She's Like the Wind"*.

* *Song written by Patrick Swayze & Stacy Widelitz.*

Morality-Challenged

Proverbs 30:20 (NKJV):
This is the way of an adulterous woman:
She eats and wipes her mouth,
And says, "I have done no wickedness."

What?! Wiping our mouths when we eat is somehow unwise and adulterous? What did she do wrong here? Ruin the nice napkin? Not leave a decent tip?

Go Sit in the Corner

Proverbs 21:9 (NKJV):
It is better to dwell in a corner of a housetop,
Than in a house with a contentious woman.

So perhaps 700 wives and 300 concubines wasn't such a Sweet Paradise after all. Maybe that's why building his house took so long. He needed to make the corners of the housetop more luxurious.

Fool's Gold

Proverbs 11:22 (RSV):
Like a gold ring in a swine's snout
is a beautiful woman without discretion.

Lesson Learned: Looks fade, but oinky-ness lasts forever.
But not in a beautiful bacony way.

Captain Lazy Makes Me Crazy

Solomon is not lazy in condemning laziness in Proverbs 10:26, 12:24, 12:27a, 15:19a, 19:24, 21:25, 22:13, 24:30-34, 26:13-16, and 28:19.

In 22:13 and 26:13, he says the sluggard's favorite excuse is: "There's a lion in the streets!" When asked to run an errand, Captain Slug'll refuse, claiming a man-eating predator is on the prowl. "Um. Did you say 'Roar!'? What about 'Grrrr!'?"

12:27a says he doesn't cook what he caught while hunting. In that case, to avoid botulism, hunt for sushi or peanut butter sandwiches.

21:25 claims a sluggard's laziness will kill him. Death by sloth? That's one laidback homicide.

Some other laaaaaazy verses:

Isn't the Phrase "Power Nap" an Oxymoron?

Proverbs 26:14 (RSV):
As the door turns on its hinges,
So does the sluggard on his bed.

And odds are, they both creak.

Labor Day

Proverbs 12:24 (NASB):
The hand of the diligent will rule,
But the slack hand will be put to forced labor.

The very thing the lazy man tries to avoid will be forced upon him: Labor!

Must Be a Heavy Spoon!

Proverbs 19:24 (NKJV):
A lazy man buries his hand in the bowl,
And will not so much as bring it to his mouth again.

How lazy can you be? Not eating food only makes you weaker.

If silverware's too heavy, try plasticware. Or drink from the bowl!

Lethargy when eating from a bowl proves especially appalling, because such laziness leads to stale soup and soggy cereal.

Even Captain Crunch can't hold out forever.

Other Proverbs:

"Let's Make a Deal!"*

* Name of a TV game show which first appeared on NBC on December 30, 1963 with host Monty Hall.

Proverbs 20:14 (NCV):
Buyers say, "This is bad. It's no good."
Then they go away
and brag about what they bought.

Heads Or Tails

Proverbs 26:4-5 (NKJV):
Do not answer a fool according to his folly,
Lest you also be like him.
Answer a fool according to his folly,
Lest he be wise in his own eyes.

When you come across a fool, flip a coin. Heads, you answer him; tails, you don't. Or as Søren Kierkegaard says: "I see it all perfectly; there are two possible situations - one can either do this or that. My honest opinion and my friendly advice is this: do it or do not do it - you will regret both."

Bitter Sweet

Proverbs 27:7 (NCV):
When you are full, not even honey tastes good,
but when you are hungry,
even something bitter tastes sweet.

So if your spouse can't cook, make sure you're especially hungry. Or order takeout. And either way, stock a healthy supply of Pepto-Bismol® and Alka-Seltzer®.

GOOD MOOOORNIIIIIIIIIIIING!!!!!!!

Proverbs 27:14 (NCV):
If you loudly greet your neighbor early in the
morning, he will think of it as a curse.

Reminds me of the "Friends" episode: "The One with All the Haste" where a happy neighbor singing "Morning's here!" annoys Rachel. "HEY!! Do you have to do that? It's Saturday!"

Intelligence-Challenged

Proverbs 30:2 (NKJV):
Surely I am more stupid than any man,
And do not have the understanding of a man.

Why do pastors always ask if this is my confirmation verse?

ECCLESISASTES

Ecclesiastes probably means "Preacher". At least that's how the author acknowledges himself. And since preacher means somebody who preaches, he lives up to his name.

The gist of Ecclesiastes? Life without God is foolish. You're going to die someday, so you'd best get right with God before you do. Or at the very least, don't upset Him too much.

If You Want Meaning in Life, Buy a Dictionary!

Ecclesiastes 1:2 (NIV):
"Meaningless! Meaningless!"
says the Teacher.
"Utterly meaningless!
Everything is meaningless."

That's what he says when he opens a box of his favorite cereal, only to find he got the same prize as last time, so he'll need to devour at least one more box in his valiant attempt to be the first on his block to collect all four.

More Is Less

Ecclesiastes 6:11 (NIV):
The more the words,
the less the meaning,
and how does that profit anyone?

David McIntoshin writing in the *National Review* (October 24, 1995): "The Lord's Prayer is 66 words, the Gettysburg Address is 286 words, there are 1,322 words in the Declaration of Independence, but government regulations on the sale of cabbage total 26,911 words."

This book contains more words than all those put together! What does that say about me?

Well, Dig This!

Ecclesiastes 10:8-9 (NKJV):
He who digs a pit will fall into it,
And whoever breaks through a wall
will be bitten by a serpent.
He who quarries stones may be hurt by them,
And he who splits wood may be endangered by it.

Well, that's encouraging.

That's why it's best to follow the safety guidelines and wear protective goggles.

All those verses do is inspire the lazy man to remain lazy, giving him more excuses not to work. As if "The spoon's too heavy" or "There's a lion outside!" weren't enough.

Babylon

Ecclesiastes 10:11 (KJV):
Surely the serpent will bite
without enchantment;
and a babbler is no better.

Some people don't understand the evil of "babble on". Those are the folks with whom you avoid making eye contact, for fear they'll recite a litany of ailments and other unpleasant diatribes in a tsunami of bitter words. If you're going to babble on, at least stay out of the other person's face. And if you can't stay back a socially-acceptable distance, at least gargle with a competent mouthwash.

Competent, meaning industrial-strength.

If a Tree Falls in the Forest ...

Ecclesiastes 11:3b (NIV):
Whether a tree falls to the south or to the north,
in the place where it falls, there will it lie.

Duh! ... Or does that mean you can't trust fallen trees?

SONG OF SONGS
(a.k.a. Song of Solomon)

Who would have thought the Bible could contain such a sexy love song? Martin Luther called this book "The High Song". But as we know today, that's incorrect. "The High Song" is something sung by Bob Marley or Cheech and Chong.

Oh Solomon, You Sweet Talker

Song of Solomon 7:2b (NKJV):
Your waist is like a heap of wheat
set about with lilies.
& 7:4b (RSV):
Your nose is like a tower of Lebanon,
overlooking Damascus.

Solomon was revered for his wisdom, as well as his romantic expertise, but I still have to ask: Are these sayings complimentary? 'Cause when I say them, I get slapped.
"A heap of what?!"

ISAIAH

I say, uh, like Joshua, Isaiah also means "Yahweh Is Salvation". Which must've caused considerable confusion amongst Old Testament messengers. "I have a message for 'Yahweh Is Salvation'." "I'm 'Yahweh Is Salvation'." "So am I." "So am I." "Looks like most of us here are named 'Yahweh Is Salvation'." "Is it a bill?" "Aye, if it's a bill, I'm not 'Yahweh Is Salvation'." "Neither am I." "Neither am I." "On second thought, looks like none of us here are named 'Yahweh Is Salvation'." "Unless it's prize money." "Aye, if it's prize money, I'm 'Yahweh Is Salvation'." "So am I." "So am I." "So am I." "So am I." "But that's more than before!" "Aye, looks like all of us here are named 'Yahweh Is Salvation'." "But only if thou bringest prize money." "We like prize money."

"Beat It!"*

* Title of 1983 song by Michael Jackson.

Isaiah 2:4b (KJV):
and they shall beat their swords into plowshares,
and their spears into pruninghooks
Joel 3:10a (KJV):
Beat your plowshares into swords
and your pruninghooks into spears
Micah 4:3b (KJV):
and they shall beat their swords into plowshares,
and their spears into pruninghooks

Imagine the blacksmiths and forgers, having just finished the laborious task of beating all the swords into plowshares and the spears into pruninghooks, being told to beat the plowshares back into swords and the pruninghooks back into spears. "What?!"

Show Me the Way, Bro

Isaiah 3:6 (ESV):
For a man will take hold of his brother
in the house of his father, saying:
"You have a cloak; you shall be our leader,
and this heap of ruins shall be under your rule";

What an offer! And yet, in the next verse, he declines that delicious deal, declaring he has neither bread nor cloak. What a joke! They want him to rule because he has a cloak. But he doesn't have a cloak. "That's a nice shirt, you wanna rule our ruins?" "No thanks. This isn't my shirt."

Don't Let This Guy Invest Your Money

Isaiah 5:10
The grain grown will be less than the seed planted! That's not a good return on your investment. Also known as a loss.

Reminds me of those ads that say: "Results may vary." Which means it won't work for you. It will only work for the happy people in the commercial.

We Have a Warm Place for You

Isaiah 14:9 (RSV):
Sheol beneath is stirred up
to meet you when you come,
it rouses the shades to greet you,
all who were leaders of the earth;
it raises from their thrones
all who were kings of the nations.

Sounds almost majestic and flattering, until you realize Sheol is the place of the dead, so you died; and in the next verse, the dead mock you as they "welcome" you to the grave. And in verse 11, maggots become your bed and worms your blanket.

So I'm guessing this room doesn't come with complimentary soaps and shampoos nor a well-stocked snack bar. And, if I were you, I wouldn't eat that "mint" on your pillow.

But isn't it cute how they folded that towel into the shape of a goat?

You Forgot Your Robe Again?!

Isaiah 20:1-3
You don't hear many, if any, sermons preached on these verses. Isaiah walked naked for three years! No boxers. No trench coat. Not even shoes! Extreme commando! Three years is too long to be considered mere streaking. So, not counting Adam and Eve, does this make Isaiah the world's first naturist?

And if he got sunburned, did he inadvertently create the first batch of hot buns?

> **How did Isaiah expect people
> to listen to his prophecies
> when they were too busy thinking:
> "Dude! Put on a loincloth!"**

It Pains Me to Say This:
Aaaaaahhhhhhhhh!!!!!!!!!!!!

Isaiah 21:3-4 (NIV):
At this my body is racked with pain,
pangs seize me, like those of a woman in labor;
I am staggered by what I hear,
I am bewildered by what I see.
My heart falters, fear makes me tremble;
the twilight I longed for has become a horror to me.

Sounds like someone needs a vacation!

This Is the Pits

Isaiah 24:18a (RSV):
He who flees at the sound of the terror
shall fall into the pit;
and he who climbs out of the pit
shall be caught in the snare.

Some days, it's best to stay in bed.
You can save time, by getting caught in the snare right away, and thus, avoid the pit.

And the Bed Bugs Probably Bite Too

Isaiah 28:20 (NIV):
The bed is too short to stretch out on,
the blanket too narrow to wrap around you.

And some days, it's best not to stay in bed.

I Didn't Do Nuttin'

Isaiah 30:7 (NCV):
to Egypt whose help is useless.
So I call that country Rahab the Do-Nothing.

Quite the insult: "the Do-Nothing". On the other hand, Rahab was a prostitute, so if she did nothing, that is, if she didn't do her job, wouldn't that be a good thing? If Isaiah means Rahab the sea monster, we want that Rahab to do nothing too.

That's like a serial killer wanting to take a vacation. "One week? Take two! Take the whole summer. I hear Antarctica's nice this time of year. Or the moon."

Smashed to Bits

Isaiah 30:14 (NIV):
It will break in pieces like pottery,
shattered so mercilessly
that among its pieces not a fragment will be found
for taking coals from a hearth
or scooping water out of a cistern."

If you wanna scoop water out of a cistern, but plan on getting that smashed, be sure you have a Designated Scooper.

Puns Ablazing

Isaiah 31:5 (NIV):
Like birds hovering overhead,
the LORD Almighty will shield Jerusalem;
he will shield it and deliver it,
he will 'pass over' it and will rescue it.

"He will 'pass over' it" -- A play on words? A good-natured allusion to The Passover?

Hay!

Isaiah 33:11 (NIV):
You conceive chaff, you give birth to straw;
your breath is a fire that consumes you.

Sounds like the one, to whom the message is given, could use a breath mint.

I'll Stop By Sometime,
When You Least Expect It!

Isaiah 37:28 (NIV):
But I know where you stay and when you
come and go and how you rage against me.

That reminds me of the threat: "I know where you live." And believe me, God knows!

God Never Loses at Hide and Seek

Isaiah 40:27 (NKJV):
Why do you say, O Jacob,
And speak, O Israel:
"My way is hidden from the LORD,
And my just claim is passed over by my God"?

Passed over again, but not in a good way. Not like last time, when being passed over was a good thing. Well, good for the Hebrews; bad for the Egyptians. Especially the firstborn.

Taking Back an Exam
Is the Only Good Definition of Detestable

Isaiah 41:24 (NIV):
But you are less than nothing and your works are utterly worthless; he who chooses you is detestable.

Less than nothing? What an insult! Like the sum of your whole existence is a negative number. You are worth less than worthless. Belly lint in the abdomen of an amoeba. A bad amoeba.

Why Would Anyone
Bow Down to Leftovers?

Isaiah 44:19 (NIV):
No one stops to think,
no one has the knowledge or understanding to say,
"Half of it [the wood from a chopped-down tree]

I used for fuel;
I even baked bread over its coals,
I roasted meat and I ate.
Shall I make a detestable thing from what is left?
Shall I bow down to a block of wood?"

Their thinking seems to be: "I'll use the scraps for kindling. If I have any wood leftover, I'll whittle that into my deity! Or an ashtray. No, wait. A wooden ashtray would be silly!"

On Second Thought, I Want the Refrigerator on the Other Side of the Kitchen

Isaiah 60:17a (NIV):
Instead of bronze I will bring you gold,
and silver in place of iron.
Instead of wood I will bring you bronze,
and iron in place of stones.

Imagine the movers carrying those things back and forth. Can't you hear them grumbling? "Bronze again?! And iron?! We just hauled those out of here; and now we've gotta bring 'em back?"

Would have been a lot easier and much quicker to leave the bronze and iron where they were; and trade wood for gold and stones for silver.

Even funnier if these movers used to be blacksmiths, but quit after that fiasco involving plowshares and spears.

"Not this again!"

JEREMIAH

Jeremiah means "Appointed by God". And just as Jeremiah was appointed by God, from time to time, he also felt disappointed.

Be Sacred, Not Scared

Jeremiah 1:17 (NIV):
Get yourself ready! Stand up and say to them whatever I command you. Do not be terrified by them, or I will terrify you before them.

Seems paradoxical that the punishment for feeling terrified is to be terrified. Like the paternal exclamation: "Don't you cry; or I'll make you cry!" That kind of punishment doesn't work with eating chocolate. "You want to eat chocolate? I'll give you chocolate to eat." "Okay. Thank you!"

The Acme god-Holder 2000 Will Keep Your god from Falling Down

Jeremiah 10:3-5 (RSV):
for the customs of the peoples are false.
A tree from the forest is cut down,
and worked with an axe by the hands of a craftsman.
Men deck it with silver and gold;
they fasten it with hammer and nails
so that it cannot move.
Their idols are like scarecrows in a cucumber field,

> and they cannot speak;
> they have to be carried, for they cannot walk.
> Be not afraid of them, for they cannot do evil,
> neither is it in them to do good."

Wooden idols can do neither good nor bad. In fact, they just sit there like logs.

Idol Thought: Why would you wanna worship a "god" that can give you splinters?

The only commands an idol obeys: Sit! Play dead. Don't let these papers blow away.

Our God Rains, Or Sunshines, Depending on the Weather

Jeremiah 10:11 (NIV):
"Tell them [the people of Israel] this: 'These gods,
who did not make the heavens and the earth,
will perish from the earth
and from under the heavens.'"*

* The text of this verse is in Aramaic.

To speakers of Aramaic (the Chaldeans), this verse says their "gods" didn't make the heavens and the earth. I.e., My God can beat up your god.

**The secular media claims the world exists
solely (or soullessly)
because of some weird cosmic accident,
but whenever there's a disaster,
they call it "an act of God".**

Farming Foibles

Jeremiah 12:13a (NIV):
They will sow wheat but reap thorns;

Maybe somebody mislabeled the seeds.

Mister Figs, You Are So Bad

Jeremiah 24:2 (KJV):
One basket had very good figs,
even like the figs that are first ripe:
and the other basket had very naughty figs,
which could not be eaten, they were so bad.

Shame on you, naughty figs!

Is that Guy ... Pregnant?

Jeremiah 30:6 (NIV):
Ask and see:
Can a man bear children?
Then why do I see every strong man
with his hands on his stomach
like a woman in labor,
every face turned deathly pale?

I know exactly what he means. I've suffered
labor pains many times myself. Usually after a
bunch of burritos with too much Tabasco sauce.

Sorry, Three Dog Night.
Jeremiah was not a bullfrog!
But Kermit was.

Not the Freedom We Wanted

Jeremiah 34:17 (NIV):
Therefore, this is what the LORD says:
You have not obeyed me; you have not proclaimed
freedom for your fellow countrymen.
So I now proclaim 'freedom' for you,
declares the LORD - 'freedom' to fall by the sword,
plague and famine. I will make you abhorrent
to all the kingdoms of the earth.

In "The Scrolls" first published in the
August 13, 1974 issue of "The New Republic" and
later released in his 1975 collection "Without
Feathers", Woody Allen wrote: "Whosoever shall
not fall by the sword or by famine, shall fall by
pestilence, so why bother shaving?"

I Ask for Freedom!
And a Bunch of Chocolate;
Not Necessarily in That Order

Jeremiah 39:11-12 (NCV):
Nebuchadnezzar king of Babylon had given
these orders about Jeremiah through Nebuzaradan,
commander of the guard:
"Find Jeremiah and take care of him.
Do not hurt him,
but do for him whatever he asks you."

But what if he asks to be set free? Or he
asks to have his country set free?

Don't Be Silly, Said Caesar, Brutus Is My Best Friend

Jeremiah 40:13-41

Johanan son of Kareah warns Gedaliah that Ishmael son of Nethaniah is coming to kill him, but Gedaliah doesn't believe him and defends Ishamel. And then Ishmael arrives and kills Gedaliah. The name Ishmael means "God sees". You'd think someone named God Sees would behave better.

If You've Seen One Pyramid, You've Seen 'Em All

Jeremiah 42:15b-17 (RSV):

... Thus says the Lord of hosts, the God of Israel:
"If you set your faces to enter Egypt
and go to live there,
then the sword which you fear
shall overtake you there in the land of Egypt;
and the famine of which you are afraid
shall follow hard after you to Egypt;
and there you shall die.
All the men who set their faces
to go to Egypt to live there
shall die by the sword, by famine, and by pestilence;
they shall have no remnant or survivor
from the evil which I will bring upon them."

Ever notice how the Egyptian Tourism Bureau never quotes those verses?

Your Pride Should Only Ween So Much

Jeremiah 48:29 (NIV):
We have heard of Moab's pride—
her overweening pride and conceit,
her pride and arrogance
and the haughtiness of her heart.

Sounds like they lack humility. But then again, humility's nothing to brag about.

Loud Braggarts

Jeremiah 48:45 (NIV):
In the shadow of Heshbon
the fugitives stand helpless,
for a fire has gone out from Heshbon,
a blaze from the midst of Sihon;
it burns the foreheads of Moab,
the skulls of the noisy boasters.

It's bad enough they boast, but they do so loudly. But then again, being quiet's nothing to shout about.

God Wins Every Time

Jeremiah 49:19b (NIV):
Who is like me and who can challenge me?
And what shepherd can stand against me?"

No one can challenge God and win. Reminds me of that "Far Side" cartoon where God is on a game show competing against a mere mortal. And, of course, God wins all the points.

Code Word: Sheshach

Jeremiah 51:41 (NIV):
How Sheshach* will be captured,
the boast of the whole earth seized!
What a horror Babylon will be among the nations!

* Sheshach is a cryptogram for Babylon.

If Sheshach is a code word for Babylon, why does he say "Babylon" in the next sentence? That gives away the meaning and ruins the reason for having a code.

If Jeremiah had a computer, his password would be: Password. His PIN? 1234.

And since his code's ineffective anyway, he might as well just say: Abylonians Bay.

Belly Lint in the Navel of a Silly Snake

Jeremiah 51:34 (NIV):
Nebuchadnezzar king of Babylon has devoured us,
he has thrown us into confusion,
he has made us an empty jar.
Like a serpent he has swallowed us
and filled his stomach with our delicacies,
and then has spewed us out.

What could be lower than snake puke? Perhaps snake puke after the serpent ate fast food.

LAMENTATIONS

Lamentations are expressions of woe. In the 1960s, expressions of woe became popular in lots of hit songs: "A woe oo, woe oo, woe oooo!"

Expressions of woe are also popular among cowboys. Especially ones with horses named Nellie.

Heartless O-Birds

Lamentations 4:3 (NIV):
Even jackals offer their breasts
to nurse their young,
but my people have become heartless
like ostriches in the desert.

Nursing jackals! Ha! I didn't know ostriches were so heartless. In need of wisdom, yes. But heartless too? How do those birds get by? Winning personalities? Not likely. They can't even fly! Not looks either. My guess? Speed and size. They're fast, big birds. And ev'ryone adores Australian accents. Good on ya', Aussie birds.

EZEKIEL

Ezekiel means "God Will Strengthen"; and you'll need God's strength to get through this book. Once you finish this book, reading the rest of the Bible seems like a breeze. But that doesn't mean Ezekiel isn't a whole lot of good, clean fun. After all, we have him to thank for inspiring the song: "Them Bones, Them Bones, Them Dry Bones". Thanks, Ezekiel!

What a Clever Name!

Ezekiel 10:13 (NKJV):
As for the wheels,
they were called in my hearing,
"Wheel."

Have No Fear

Ezekiel 11:8 (NIV):
You fear the sword, and the sword is what I will bring against you, declares the Sovereign LORD.

Just as in Job 3:25, what you fear comes upon you, so you might as well fear something comfy. Which would you rather say? "Yikes! The sword which I feared has come upon me." or "Alas, the soft pillows which I feared have come upon me."

Forget the Frying Pan, This Is:
Out of the Fire and Into the Fire

Ezekiel 15:2-5 (NIV):
"Son of man,
how is the wood of a vine
different from that of a branch
from any of the trees in the forest?

Is wood ever taken from it to make anything useful?
Do they make pegs from it to hang things on?
And after it is thrown on the fire as fuel
and the fire burns both ends
and chars the middle,
is it then useful for anything?
If it was not useful for anything
when it was whole, how much less
can it be made into something useful
when the fire has burned it
and it is charred?

The wood of the vine is only "good" for fuel. But even as fuel, it's bad. That's like those whose only "talent" is singing. But even then, they still can't carry a tune. You see folks like that at tryouts for "American Idol" and at karaoke.

Sorry Sisters

Ezekiel 16

God raises Jerusalem from a helpless infant to a grown woman who repays His love by cheating on Him every chance she gets.

In Verse 20, God admonishes her for taking the children she bore to Him and sacrificing them as food for her idols. He even asks, "Wasn't your prostitution bad enough?"

Verses 31b-34: You differed from a hooker, because you refused payment. You adulterous wife, who takes strangers instead of her husband! Whores take money from their customers, but you pay yours! You hire them from all over to fulfill your illicit desires. In that you are the opposite of a prostitute, because no one hires you; you hire them!

In verses 47-48, the LORD chides Jerusalem for becoming even more evil than her sister Sodom.

Like the Elvis song "Little Sister" (written by Jerome "Doc" Pomus & Mort Shuman) says: "Little sister don't you do what your big sister done."

He Named His Dog "Dog"

Ezekiel 20:29 (NIV):
Then I said to them:
What is this high place you go to?
(It is called Bamah* to this day.)"

* The footnote says: Bamah means high place.

They called the high place "high place". That's sooooooo clever.

A Cast of Thousands

Ezekiel 30:22 (NIV):
Therefore this is what the Sovereign LORD says:
I am against Pharaoh king of Egypt.
I will break both his arms,
the good arm as well as the broken one,
and make the sword fall from his hand.

Sounds like both arms get broken, but one gets broken twice.

Integrity-Challenged

Ezekiel 38:13 (NIV):
Sheba and Dedan and the merchants of Tarshish
and all her villages will say to you,
"Have you come to plunder?
Have you gathered your hordes to loot,
to carry off silver and gold,
to take away livestock and goods
and to seize much plunder?"

I'm guessing their answer will be no. "Us plunder? Our hordes loot? What kind of hordes do you take us for?" Why would Sheba and Dedan ask such a question? Of course, the people of Gog are going to deny it. There's no honor among thieves.

<u>DANIEL</u>

Daniel means "God Is My Judge". And Dan the Man survives the Lion's Den like no one else can! And like Joey before him, Oh Danny Boy interprets dreams fore-fun and prophet.

Name Dropping

Daniel 1:6 (NKJV):
Now from among those of the sons of Judah
were Daniel, Hananiah, Mishael, and Azariah.

Having a catchier name like Daniel will help you be remembered longer. And they'll name the

book after you too. That's why Leslie Townes
Hope changed his name to Bob; Amos Alphonsus
Muzyad Yakhoob changed his name to Danny
Thomas; Joseph Levitch changed his name to Jerry
Lewis; and Cornelius Crane Chase changed his
name to Chevy. That worked for Hananiah,
Mishael, and Azariah to a degree too, since most
people know them better by their new names:
"Shadrach, Meshach, and Abed-Nego".

Going Veggie!

Daniel 1:12 (NKJV):
Please test your servants for ten days,
and let them give us vegetables to eat
and water to drink.

Are these guys the world's first vegetarians?
If only more people would become
vegetarians, we'd get seated quicker at the
steakhouse.

The Wisest of Idiots
Is Still an Idiot

Daniel 2:12 (NIV):
This made the king so angry and furious
that he ordered the execution
of all the wise men of Babylon.

Killing all the wise people is not a good
idea. 'Cause all you're left with are foolish folks.

Strike Up the Band

Daniel 3:5 (NIV):
"As soon as you hear the sound of the horn, flute,
zither, lyre, harp, pipes and all kinds of music,
you must fall down and worship the image of gold
that King Nebuchadnezzar has set up."

A running gag! The phrase "the sound of
the horn, flute, zither, lyre, harp, pipes and all kinds
of music" gets repeated over and over again. They
couldn't just say "When the band plays"? Like the
pilot episode of "Fawlty Towers" ("A Touch of
Class") where Mister Wareing keeps repeating his
unfilled drink order: "A gin and orange, a lemon
squash, and a scotch and water please!"

Knee-Knockers

Daniel 5:6 (NIV):
His face turned pale and he was so frightened
that his knees knocked together
and his legs gave way.

Made me laugh when Don Knotts did that.

You Look Like You Need
an SPF of at Least 45

Daniel 5:10b (NIV):
"O king, live forever!" she said.
"Don't be alarmed! Don't look so pale!"

In other words, stop being such a wuss!

HOSEA

Like Joshua and Isaiah, Hosea also means "Yahweh Is Salvation". Back then, when anyone in a crowd called out, "Yahweh Is Salvation!", more than forty people replied, "Yes?"

Your Momma's Calling You!

Hosea 1:4-9

First, God makes Hosea marry a harlot. Then He tells him to name his children "God plants", "No-Mercy", and "Not-My-People". (Jezreel means God plants; Lo-Ruhamah means no mercy; and Lo-Ammi means not my people.)

I wonder what Hosea's neighbors thought when they heard this: "Hey God Plants! Hey Not Loved! Hey Not My People! You kids better hurry home; your momma's lookin' for you!"

How About a Spritz
of Morning Mist?

Hosea 6:4b (NIV):
Your love is like the morning mist,
like the early dew that disappears.

Love like the Morning Mist? That's not the kind of love most people want.

In "The Trip (Part 1)" episode of "Seinfeld",

George Costanza says he dresses according to his mood. When Jerry asks what mood George is wearing, George replies, "Morning Mist."

Suddenly, I No Longer Feel Inspired

Hosea 9:7b (NIV):
Because your sins are so many
and your hostility so great,
the prophet is considered a fool,
the inspired man a maniac.

If a maniac becomes unhappy, does that make him maniac depressive?

Instead of antidepressants, why don't doctors prescribe pro-happies?

I'll See You in Court!
(I Mean the Food Court)

Hosea 10:4 (NIV):
They make many promises, take false oaths and
make agreements; therefore lawsuits spring up
like poisonous weeds in a plowed field.

"Lawsuits springing up" sounds like punishment to me. Especially lawsuits "like poisonous weeds in a plowed field." That sounds so lyrical, you can almost dance to it.

Why are all lawyers from Pennsylvania? They always say "Attorneys at law, P.A." But that's okay, 'cause all the doctors are from Maryland.

I Can't Find the Exit!

Hosea 13:13 (NIV):
Pains as of a woman in childbirth come to him,
but he is a child without wisdom;
when the time arrives,
he does not come to the opening of the womb.

Hey kid, follow the Light! Don't be scared.
No one's gonna slap you. (Snicker, twitter, giggle.)

Cindy Byrnes O'Halloran asks:
"Is that where the saying,
'light at the end of the tunnel' comes from?"

JOEL

Joel means "Yahweh Is God". Although over 18 when he wrote this book, he's still considered a Minor Prophet.

Honey?
Did You Put Out Plenty of
No-Pest Strips?

Joel 1:4 (NIV):
What the locust swarm has left
the great locusts have eaten;
what the great locusts have left
the young locusts have eaten;
what the young locusts have left
other locusts have eaten.

If one locust doesn't get you, another one will. Good for the locusts; bad for you. What a horrible plague! People don't want all they hold dear turned into Purina Locust Chow.

That's My Favorite Shirt!

Joel 2:13a (NIV):
Rend your heart and not your garments.

Garments cost money to mend. But hearts can be changed for free. Kneel before the Lord; and let Him make the necessary altar-ations.

AMOS

Amos means "Burden". Or it could be the singular form of mosses. As in, "Do you want two mosses?" "No, thank you. I just want Amos."

Amos uses this phrase a lot: "For three sins of _____, even for four, I will not turn back my wrath." And those whose fury flames unchecked will have fire sent upon them. That's why it's best to keep your fury at a comfortable temperature.

Divine Comedy

Amos 3:3-6 (NIV):
Do two walk together
unless they have agreed to do so?
Does a lion roar in the thicket
when he has no prey?

Does he growl in his den
when he has caught nothing?
Does a bird fall into a trap on the ground
where no snare has been set?
Does a trap spring up from the earth
when there is nothing to catch?
When a trumpet sounds in a city,
do not the people tremble?
When disaster comes to a city,
has not the LORD caused it?

I don't know if a lion growls in his den if he's caught nothing, but I'm sure his stomach does.

"Just When You Thought It Was Safe"*

* Tagline for the 1978 movie "JAWS 2".

Amos 5:19 (NIV):
It will be as though a man fled from a lion
only to meet a bear,
as though he entered his house
and rested his hand on the wall
only to have a snake bite him.

"Yay! I escaped the lion. Oh-Oh! Dancing Bear doesn't wanna dance; he's hungry!"

What kind of house has snakes waiting for you to rest a hand on the wall so they can bite you!

"Whew! Now that I got away from that lion and bear, I'll just rest my hand here on this snake-infested wall." (Hiss! Chomp!) "Ow! I should never have bought Junior that pregnant king cobra."

God Adds Comedy Writer
to His Already Extensive Résumé

From Amos 6:12 (ESV):
Does one plow there* with oxen?

* The footnote says: "Or *the sea*".

God makes a joke! "Does one plow the sea with oxen?" That's some kind of comedy. Clash of Contexts? What other deities are that much fun? (None. Because there are no other deities. Duh!)

Call Waiting

Amos 7:14-15 (NIV)
Amos answered Amaziah, "I was neither a prophet nor the son of a prophet, but I was a shepherd, and I also took care of sycamore-fig trees.
But the LORD took me
from tending the flock and said to me,
'Go, prophesy to my people Israel.'

God calls unwilling prophets; 'cause even He wonders about the ones who want that kind of calling.

<u>OBADIAH</u>

Obadiah means "Servant of God". But his name could also be the response you give when you've been caught doing something wrong. "Aha! I caught you!" "Oh bad, I, uh!"

Maybe not. Not a man of many words, he wrote one chapter, a mere 21 verses.

Beware of Thieves and Robbers Who Steal

Obadiah 5 (NIV):
"If thieves came to you, if robbers in the night—
Oh, what a disaster awaits you—
would they not steal only as much as they wanted?
If grape pickers came to you,
would they not leave a few grapes?

God says through Obadiah that even thieves and robbers would leave something, but He won't, not when He fully destroys the people of Edom. But too bad that when He wiped out the Edomites, He didn't destroy the termites too. Wood dent you?

JONAH

Jonah means "Dove". At least his name meant that back then. Nowadays his name means a bringer of bad luck. But if Jonah wanted to win popularity contests, he wouldn't have majored in Doomsday Prophecies. With a minor in Feeding Marine Life.

**Give a man a fish;
and you feed him for a day.
But give him a whale;
and you'll feed him for weeks.**

Something Smells Fishy

Jonah 1
The main god of Nineveh was Dagon, the fish-god. After Jonah refused to warn the Ninevites to turn from worshipping their false fish god, he gets swallowed by a real great fish!

You Feeling Okay, Jonah?
You Smell Like Fish Puke

Jonah 2:10-3:3a (NIV):
And the LORD commanded the fish,
and it vomited Jonah onto dry land.
Then the word of the LORD
came to Jonah a second time:
"Go to the great city of Nineveh
and proclaim to it the message I give you."
Jonah obeyed the word of the LORD
and went to Nineveh.

You bet he obeyed! He got puked out of a great fish for disobeying the first time, you can be sure he obeyed the second time. I wonder how many people offered him a Breath Mint?

MICAH

Micah means "Who Is Like God?" which is meant to emphasize the uniqueness of God. Micah's own uniqueness shines forth so much that I bill him as: "The Punster Prophet". He uses a lot of plays on words, which unfortunately lose their luster in translation. I.e., in 1:10, he tells the people who live in Beth Aphrah (which means "House of Dust") to roll themselves in the dust. In 1:11 (NKJV): "the inhabitant of Zaanan ('Going Out') does not go out." In 1:14 (NKJV): "The houses of Achzib ('Lie') shall be a lie to the kings of Israel." 1:15 (NKJV): "I will yet bring an heir to you, O inhabitant of Mareshah ('Inheritance')."

There Is No 'I' in Team,
But There Are Four in Mississippi*

My spoof of a quote by Michael Jordan.

Micah 1:13a (NIV):
You who live in Lachish*,
harness the team to the chariot.

* Lachish sounds like the Hebrew for team.

Typical of the puns he pens. Some consider puns to be the lowest form of humor. But anything God does is of the highest quality. Thus, this is the highest form of the lowest form of humor.

Thanks for Playing

Micah 1:14 (ESV):
Therefore you shall give parting gifts
to Moresheth-gath;

Parting gifts? Sounds like a game show. "That's right, Bob! Moresheth-gath will receive coupons for food they can't stand, subscriptions to magazines they won't read, and the home version of our game show so they can play along at home."

Just Say No
To Negativity!

Micah 2:6 (ESV):
"Do not preach"—thus they preach—
"one should not preach of such things;
    disgrace will not overtake us."

They preach, "Don't preach!" How effective is that? Might as well protest against protests and speak out against speaking out. Cease cessations!

Or like Mitch Hedberg says: "I'm against picketing. … But I don't know how to show it."

Dry Humor

Micah 6:10 (NIV):
Am I still to forget, O wicked house,
your ill-gotten treasures and the short ephah*,
        which is accursed?

* An ephah was a dry measure.

The dry measure part isn't funny, per se. (Maybe if you say it fifty times fast while juggling squeaking rubber ducks. A funny accent helps too.)

But the idea of God forgetting is humorous.

Like The All-Knowing could misplace his car keys. (For His Infinity.)

"Now where did I put that planet I created with all those rebellious people?"

No Spread for You!

Micah 6:15 (The Message):
You'll plant grass but never get a lawn.
You'll make jelly but never spread it on your bread.
You'll press apples but never drink the cider.

NAHUM

Nahum means "Comforter". But his idea of comforting is to warn about the forthcoming wrath of God. "God will destroy you wicked unbelievers! ... Sweet dreams."

You Throw Like a Girl!

Nahum 3:13a (NIV):
Look at your troops— they are all women!

Back then, that was considered an insult. Like back when one football team would say another team played like a bunch of girls.

HABAKKUK

Habakkuk means "Embrace"; so if you like to hug, you could call yourself a Habakkukian.
Or not.
'Cause that sounds kooky; and looks hard to spell.

Keep Quiet

Habakkuk 2:18-19 (NKJV):
"What profit is the image, that its maker should carve it,
The molded image, a teacher of lies,
That the maker of its mold should trust in it,
To make mute idols?
Woe to him who says to wood, 'Awake!'
To silent stone, 'Arise! It shall teach!'
Behold, it is overlaid with gold and silver,
Yet in it there is no breath at all.

Woe to him who says to wood, "Awake!"
Woe and a straightjacket.
Before whom do they bow?
… A stack of Purina Termite Chow!

Hi Hills! How's It Going?

Habakkuk 3:19 (NKJV):
The LORD God is my strength;
He will make my feet like deer's feet,
And He will make me walk on my high hills.

When you sing this, annunciate carefully, or it'll sound like you're singing "And He will make me walk on my high heels."

ZEPHANIAH

Zephaniah means "He Whom Yahweh Has Hidden". Containing only 3-chapters and 53-verses, this book remains somewhat hidden.

And yet, it's well worth finding, since 3:17b says the LORD will quiet us with His love and rejoice over us with singing.

God will serenade us!

What a sweet thought!

And so's the fact that we're almost to the Not As Ancient Testament!

God loves me!
Who am I to disagree?

Maintain a Firm Grip at All Times

Zephaniah 3:16 (NIV):
On that day they will say to Jerusalem,
"Do not fear, O Zion;
do not let your hands hang limp.

Not the 3:16 we usually hear about. Certainly not one seen at sporting events. Although this one seems better suited for athletics than John's.

<u>HAGGAI</u>

Haggai means "My Holiday" or "My Feast", but that doesn't mean this book's a picnic. Mr. My Holiday calls us to action, to work, to build for God! And when we build for God, we'd better build something huge, because He owns a lot of stuff!

Concentrate on Consecration

Haggai 2:11-19 (NIV):
"This is what the LORD Almighty says:
'Ask the priests what the law says:
If a person carries consecrated meat
in the fold of his garment,
and that fold touches some bread or stew,
some wine, oil or other food,
does it become consecrated?'"
The priests answered, "No."
Then Haggai said, "If a person defiled by contact
with a dead body touches one of these things,
does it become defiled?"
"Yes," the priests replied, "it becomes defiled."
Then Haggai said, "'So it is with this people
and this nation in my sight,' declares the LORD.
'Whatever they do
and whatever they offer there is defiled.
Now give careful thought to this from this day on
—consider how things were before one stone
was laid on another in the LORD's temple.
When anyone came to a heap of twenty measures,
there were only ten.
When anyone went to a wine vat
to draw fifty measures, there were only twenty.
I struck all the work of your hands with blight,
mildew and hail, yet you did not turn to me,'
declares the LORD. 'From this day on,
from this twenty-fourth day of the ninth month,
give careful thought to the day when the foundation
of the LORD's temple was laid.

Give careful thought:
Is there yet any seed left in the barn?
Until now, the vine and the fig tree,
the pomegranate and the olive tree
have not borne fruit.
"'From this day on I will bless you.'"

Lesson Learned: Being cursed is the worst, but being blest is the best. Cha-ching! Um, I mean, Hallelujah!

ZECHARIAH

Zechariah means "Jehovah Remembers". The eleventh of the twelve minor prophets. Twelve minor prophets are what you get when kids run a dozen little lemonade stands. Zechariah's ministry took place during the reign of Darius the Great. As opposed to Marvin the Mediocre or Olaf the Okeydokey.

Don't You Know?

Zechariah 4:11-13 (NIV):
Then I asked the angel, "What are these two olive trees on the right and the left of the lampstand?" Again I asked him, "What are these two olive branches beside the two gold pipes that pour out golden oil?" He replied, "Do you not know what these are?" "No, my lord," I said.

Of course he doesn't know! He just asked twice what they are.

<u>MALACHI</u>

Malachi means "My Messenger". Before the USPS, UPS, and Fed-Ex, there were prophets and angels. God's messengers. And when God cared enough to send the very best, He didn't wander around a Hallmark store searching for the right card. He sent His Son! But sadly, most of the world replied, "Return To Sender!"

Is This the Best You Have to Offer?

Malachi 1:8 (NKJV):
"'And when you offer the blind as a sacrifice,
is it not evil?
And when you offer the lame and sick, is it not evil?
Offer it then to your governor!
Would he be pleased with you?
Would he accept you favorably?'
says the LORD of hosts."

Like in some old comedy from last century where the mother visits her son and says, "When the Queen of England visits, she gets paper plates too?"

"I read the Bible religiously."

"But why read the Bible over and over again? God's Word never changes."

"Yes, It does. It changes me. Every time I read It."

THE NOT AS ANCIENT TESTAMENT

MATTHEW

Matthew means "Gift of God". Nickname: Matt. Before you enter the house of God, wipe your spiritual feet on this Mat.

Isn't There a McDonald's Around Here?

Matthew 4:2 (NKJV):
And when He had fasted forty days and forty nights,
afterward He was hungry.

Duh!

Reel Men

Matthew 4:19 (NASB):
And He [Jesus] said to them
[Simon (Peter) and Andrew],
"Follow Me, and I will make you fishers of men."

An old joke talks about a man seeing Billy Graham with some gorgeous gals and saying: "If you're fishing for men, you're using the right bait."

Give a man a fish;
and you feed him for a day.
But teach a man to fish;
and you won't see him all weekend.

Pace Yourself

Matthew 5:9 (NIV):
Blessed are the peacemakers,
for they will be called sons of God.

I try to read without my glasses as often as I can. But when I read that verse, I have to stop and wonder, why is Jesus blessing the pacemakers?

"Hey Right Hand, What Are You Doing?" "I Can't Tell You, Lefty"

Matthew 6:2 (NASB):
So when you give to the poor,
do not sound a trumpet before you,
as the hypocrites do in the synagogues and
in the streets, so that they may be honored by men.
Truly I say to you, they have their reward in full.

Unable to afford trumpets, the poorer hypocrites used kazoos.

Zombie Funeral Workers

Matthew 8:22 (NKJV):
But Jesus said to him,
"Follow Me, and let the dead bury their own dead."

It's not every day you see grave-digging corpses. They'd be pretty handy though. They could dig their own graves and plop right in. Kudos if they can cover themselves too.

The Illustrious Eleventh Commandment

Matthew 15:11 (NKJV):
"Not what goes into the mouth defiles a man;
but what comes out of the mouth,
this defiles a man."

When I was in third grade, my Mom asked if I washed my hands for dinner; and I hadn't, so I quoted her that Bible verse. But I wound up washing my hands that night. Because she quoted the Ten Commandments and played the "honor your father and mother" card. She also created an Eleventh Commandment: "Thou shalt wash thine hands; or thou shalt hunger greatly. Thee; and thine cattle, for a thousand generations."

Blind Weeds

Matthew 15:13-14 (NIV):
He [Jesus] replied,
"Every plant that my heavenly Father has not
planted will be pulled up by the roots.
Leave them; they are blind guides.
If a blind man leads a blind man,
both will fall into a pit."

Having Mustered My Beliefs,
I Relish the Faith I Have

Matthew 17:20 (NKJV):
So Jesus said to them,
"Because of your unbelief;

for assuredly, I say to you,
if you have faith as a mustard seed,
you will say to this mountain,
'Move from here to there,' and it will move;
and nothing will be impossible for you.

My pastor said to be saved, all I need is the faith of a mustard seed; and that's great, because, I believe in mustard.   I believe it goes well with ketchup and tastes good on hot dogs and burgers.

He talks so much about mustard, because he worked at McDonald's to get through seminary. When you have a problem, he says: "Let's McPray."

He makes Communion a Happy Meal.

And he Super-Sizes his sermons.

**Having the faith of a mustard seed
doesn't mean you should act
like a holy hot dog.**

Evil Spirits Be Gone!*

* Evil Spirits Be Gone! Sounds like exorcism in a convenient, handy dandy spray can.

Matthew 17:21

Jesus says a certain kind of demon won't go out, except by prayer and fasting.

Then I'm in trouble, 'cause I've got a chocolate peanut butter pie!

Why do they call it fasting, when it feels like it lasts forever?

Maybe it's a contraction of forever lasts.

Do you know which demon is best cast out by fasting? ... Yep! The demon of gluttony.

I tried to fast and pray. But I got hungry. The demon of chocolate chip cookies got a hold of me and wouldn't let go, until I drowned 'im in milk.

A House, Not a Den; for Prayer, Not Thievery

Matthew 21:13 (NKJV):
And He [Jesus] said to them
[those who bought and sold in the Temple],
"It is written, 'My house shall be called a house of prayer,' but you have made it a 'den of thieves.'"

While in elementary school, I went up to my Mom when she volunteered to sell Sunday School supplies at church; and I quoted her that verse.

She explained how selling Sunday School supplies wasn't the same as the atrocities committed by the people Jesus drove out of the Temple.

Probably because the people in the Temple didn't have bookshelves and a nice glass case.

Wretches Beware!

Matthew 21:41a (NIV):
He will bring those wretches to a wretched end

What other end would a wretch expect?

**How did Mary make the Messiah's sash?
... She cross-stitched.**

Lots O' Woes

Matthew Chapter 23
Jesus condemns the Pharisees and the teachers of the law with quite a bit of humor. Verse 24's my favorite (NKJV): "Blind guides, who strain out a gnat and swallow a camel!"

"Help! Hymie needs the Heimlich! He swallowed a camel!"

"Good thing he strained out those gnats."

Title Goes Here!

Matthew 27:17 (RSV):
So when they had gathered,
Pilate said to them,
"Whom do you want me to release for you,
Barabbas
or Jesus who is called Christ?"

The word Christ is the Greek form of the Jewish word Messiah, which means "The Anointed One". Christ is Jesus' title, not His last name. Joseph and Mary didn't have a sign on their front door that read: "The Christ's".

**I know we should take the Gospel
to where people gather.
But I still feel weird
worshipping at a place called
Joe's Sporting Goods
and
Community Church.**

Night of the Walking Dead

Matthew 27:52-53 (NIV):
The tombs broke open and the bodies of
many holy people who had died were raised to life.
They came out of the tombs,
and after Jesus' resurrection they went
into the holy city and appeared to many people.

If anything was funny about this, it'd have to
be the looks on the faces of the folks who saw this
happen. "Hey, Morty. I thought you were dead."
"I was. But I got over it."

**When you consider how much agony
Jesus suffered for our sins,
you can't accuse God of nepotism.**

For Sale:
One Tomb,
Slightly Used

Matthew 28
Do you know Jesus rose from the dead? I'm
sure you've heard about it. It's been the biggest
newsflash for the last two thousand years. But do
you know it?
Have you heard the Swoon Theory? The
theory that Jesus passed out on the cross, came to in
the tomb, and then claimed He conquered Death.
(Yawns.) "I had the worst nightmare ever."
(Looks at wrists/hands. Gulps.) "Oh, no I didn't."

(Realization. Gasps.) "I conquered Death!" (Walks forward; stops.) "A little help please. There's a big boulder blocking the exit."

That's not what happened. That's not the Jesus I know. Sure, He was tired. They kept Him awake all night. But He didn't stretch out on the cross and decide to take an afternoon snooze.

"I forgiveth thee. Now 'tis time for my power nap."

You can't sleep on a cross. Not just because of excruciating pain, splinters, and lack of a pillow. If you pass out, you're dead. The Nap that Never Ends. If you're not able to push yourself up to breathe, you suffocate. And that's bad. That's why the soldiers broke the legs of the criminals. Nothing hastens death faster than suffocation. Except for a bomb hidden in someone's Stromboli. Bomboli?

How convincing of a Conqueror Over Death can one be after being tortured and stuck in a cave without food, drink, light, fresh air, or medical attention for a couple nights?

How do you roll away a boulder by yourself? Especially from inside, which is against the groove! Where you can't get any leverage. And you've suffered puncture wounds in all your extremities.

Having had nails driven through your feet, how compelling does this sound?:

(Holds out hands majestically.) "Rejoice!" (Steps on sore foot.) "Ow! I've conquered." (Steps on other sore foot.) "Ow! Death." (Steps on first sore foot again.) "Yeeow! Oh, the agony." (Hops on other sore foot, trips, and falls facedown.)

That's still not the Jesus I know. And that's hardly the inspiring speech that led the disciples to die spreading the Gospel!

So clearly, Jesus died on the cross. Most secular scholars acknowledge that fact. They also acknowledge the empty tomb. Even the enemies of Christ acknowledged the empty tomb!

The elders and chief priests met to come up with a plan: Bribe the soldiers to have them claim they fell asleep; and as they slept, the disciples stole Jesus' body. Like some kind of crazy corpse kleptomaniacs. Nocturnal cadaver-nappers!

That was their brilliant plan! But it doesn't make sense. If the soldiers were asleep, how would they know what happened? Or whom at the tomb did what? (That's like the way the "Important Safety Information" for a certain sleep-aid says: "Sleepwalking, and eating or driving while not fully awake, with amnesia for the event, have been reported. If you experience any of these behaviors contact your provider immediately." How can you report it? If you don't remember it happening?)

Besides, the disciples were scared. Too scared to take on Roman soldiers. And yet, after the resurrection, the disciples boldly proclaimed they saw Jesus alive! Their proclamation became the cornerstone of the Christian faith. And unlike televangelists today, they didn't make mounds of money.

All the disciples, except Judas Iscariot and John, were tortured and killed, martyred for their faith; and yet, none wavered from acknowledging the truth that they had seen Jesus alive. Judas killed himself before Jesus rose from the dead. And John was exiled to the Island of Patmos where he wrote The Revelation of Jesus Christ. Even throughout his long life, John never wavered from proclaiming Jesus rose from the dead. None of the disciples ever said, "We were just kidding. Good one, huh?"

James, the half-brother of Jesus, who didn't believe in Jesus before the resurrection, afterwards became head of the church and proclaimed Jesus rose from the dead.

Paul, who persecuted the early church, saw Jesus alive and became Christianity's most famous missionary.

As Lee Strobel states in "The Case for the Real Jesus", most secular scholars acknowledge these five facts: Jesus died on the cross. His tomb became empty. The disciples proclaimed Jesus resurrected. James' change of heart. And Paul's change of heart. The only event that best explains all five facts is that Christ conquered Death. Jesus didn't just resuscitate. He didn't just come back to life. He conquered Death!

Wow! Why do I suddenly feel like I should sing a hymn? At least take up an offering! (Sing): "Amazing Grace, how sweet the sound, that saved a wretch like"* that guy! (Point indiscriminately. You don't want to hurt anyone's feelings. And you don't want to get beat up. Not necessarily in that order.) (Say): What? The Bible says we're all wretched, because of our sin. (Roll your eyes and tilt your head toward the imaginary "wretched guy".) Just some seem more so than others.

From "Amazing Grace" written by John Newton.

**Christian books
are cross-referenced.**

MARK

Mark means "large hammer". So when you read his Gospel, it's "Hammer Time!"*

From MC Hammer's 1990 hit signature song "U Can't Touch This!"

Which
Is Easier to Say?

Mark 2:9 (NIV):
"Which is easier:
to say to the paralytic, 'Your sins are forgiven,'
or to say, 'Get up, take your mat and walk'?"

I'm gonna go with: "Your sins are forgiven." 'Cause it has less syllables. Besides, with all those T's, "Get up, take your mat and walk" might make you spit. But both are a lot easier to say than: "Peter Piper picked a peck of pickled peppers."*

Traditional English nursery rhyme.

Don't forget to floss your soul!

And These Little Piggies
Went Wee-Wee-Wee
All the Way
Off the Cliff*

* *My variation of a traditional nursery rhyme.*

Mark 5:1-17
Jesus casts a legion of demons out of a man. The demons flee into a large herd of pigs and causes them to rush into the lake and drown. When those who live around there hear what happened, they plead with Jesus to leave their region. Lesson Learned: If you don't want people to beg you to leave, don't mess with their bacon!

"The Dancing Queen"*
(A.k.a. The Boogie-Woogie Princess)

* *Title of a 1976 song by Swedish pop group ABBA.*

Mark 6:21-28
Salome [the daughter of Herodias; the Jewish historian Flavius Josephus gave us her name] dances so well for King Herod ,that he offers her anything she wants, up to half his kingdom. Now that had to be some dance! Probably not a liturgical dance. Nothing churchy about it. (And I'm sure she prefers to be called an exotic dancer, instead of the more likely name.) So Salome asks her mother Herodias what she should get. Her mommy tells her to ask for the head of John the

Baptist.   Salome's gotta be thinking, "Yuck!   I didn't do all my best dance moves for the severed head of some prophet."

So what does she ask for? The head of John the Baptist, but she specifies she wants his head on a platter.   So she gets a platter;   mommy gets a head; and Herod's organization becomes non-prophet.

Be sure to try New and Improved Heaven!
Now with fluffier clouds and shinier halos.
And for your convenience,
we made eternity fifteen minutes longer.

"Our Lips Are Sealed"*

* Title of a 1981 song by The Go-Go's.

Mark 9:33-34 (NIV):
They [Jesus and the disciples] came to Capernaum.
When he [Jesus] was in the house,
he asked them [the disciples],
"What were you arguing about on the road?"
But they kept quiet because on the way
they had argued about who was the greatest.

Usually, when people don't want to talk to God, it's because of something they've done wrong.

Don't we all want to talk to the boss after we know we've done something right? Maybe hint at possible promotions and raises. See what we can pick from the Catalog of Miracles.

The Sad You Sees

Mark 12:24 (NIV):
Jesus replied, "Are you not in error
because you do not know
the Scriptures or the power of God?"

What a polite way of telling the Sadducees that they are so incorrect, misguided, mistaken, erroneous, inaccurate, false, faulty, flawed, fallacious, unfounded, off beam, wide of the mark, spot-off, in left field at the wrong ballpark, not in the same cemetery as dead-on. Um, wrong!

Wrong Answer!

Mark 12:27 (NIV):
"He is not the God of the dead,
but of the living.
You are badly mistaken!"

Jesus tells the Sadducees that not only are they mistaken, they're badly mistaken. Which is way worse than being goodly mistaken. Or even merely mistaken.

So I guess there's a good mistaken and a bad mistaken. An example of being goodly mistaken might be putting too much whipped cream on a piece of pie.

Ha! As if there were such a thing!

**Get right with God;
or be left with Satan.**

LUKE

Luke means "Light-Giving". So if you want to brighten your life: Take a look at Luke.

One Syllable.
Sounds Like ...

Luke 1:62 (NIV):
Then they made signs to his father,
to find out what he would like to name the child.

Why?! Why did they make signs to him? Zechariah was mute, not deaf. If only he could talk, he'd have told them so himself. Maybe he rolled his eyes at their attempts to communicate through signs instead of just talking to him. I wonder if they wrote to him in Braille.

No Woe for You!

Luke 6:25b (NKJV):
Woe to you who laugh now,
For you shall mourn and weep.

This passage doesn't condemn all laughter. Taken in context, those words condemn those laughing at Jesus, but not at His jokes, at his teaching, with mocking laughter, not holy laughter.
So laugh to your heart's content.
There's no woe for you.
Unless you stole this book.

I Thought I Saw Dust; That's Right, Sawdust

Luke 6:41-42 (NIV):
"Why do you look at
the speck of sawdust in your brother's eye
and pay no attention to the plank in your own eye?
How can you say to your brother,
'Brother, let me take the speck out of your eye,'
when you yourself
fail to see the plank in your own eye?
You hypocrite, first take the plank out of your eye,
and then you will see clearly
to remove the speck from your brother's eye.

Carpenter comedy.

**When Jesus carried lumber for Joseph,
He was cross training.**

Touched by a Sinner

Luke 7:47 (NIV):
"Therefore, I tell you, her many sins
have been forgiven—for she loved much.
But he who has been forgiven little loves little."

That doesn't mean we should sin a bunch, just so we'll love Jesus more. Although taken out of context, one might think, "I wanna love Jesus more, so I'm gonna rob a liquor store!"

Hey Fred,
You Awake?

Luke 11:5-8 (NIV):
Then Jesus said to them [His disciples],
"Suppose you have a friend,
and you go to him at midnight and say,
'Friend, lend me three loaves of bread;
a friend of mine on a journey has come to me,
and I have no food to offer him.'
And suppose the one inside answers,
'Don't bother me. The door is already locked,
and my children and I are in bed.
I can't get up and give you anything.'
I tell you, even though
he will not get up and give you the bread
because of friendship,
yet because of your shameless audacity
he will surely get up
and give you as much as you need.

A shameless plug for shameless audacity.

Insert Clever Heading Here

Luke 11:19-20 (NIV):
"Now if I drive out demons by Beelzebub,
by whom do your followers drive them out?
So then,
they will be your judges.
But if I drive out demons by the finger of God,
then the kingdom of God has come to you."

I don't think their followers drove out demons, which makes Jesus' admonition, that they'd be their judges, humorous. By whom do your followers drive out demons? Oh, that's right. They don't! So don't bad-mouth The One Who does.

"Well, Excuuuuuuuuuuuuuussssssssse Me!"*

* One of Steve Martin's iconic catchphrases.

Luke 14:18-20 (NIV):
"But they all alike began to make excuses.
The first said, 'I have just bought a field,
and I must go and see it. Please excuse me.'
Another said, 'I have just bought five yoke of oxen,
and I'm on my way to try them out.
Please excuse me.'
Still another said, 'I just got married,
so I can't come.'"

Excuses, excuses, excuses! And none of them hold up. It's a meal, not orders to move to a foreign country. The first guy can see his new field after the banquet. Besides, it'll be a lot easier to see the next day when the sun shines. Why did he buy it if he hadn't already seen it?

The second guy can try out his oxen later. That'll be easier to do during daylight too.

And the third guy? Sure, he just got married. But they've gotta eat some time. Bring her along. Free date!

Hey, Look!
There Goes Mister Tower-Unfinisher!

Luke 14:28-30 (NIV):
"Suppose one of you wants to build a tower.
Will he not first sit down and estimate the cost
to see if he has enough money to complete it?
For if he lays the foundation
and is not able to finish it,
everyone who sees it will ridicule him, saying,
'This fellow began to build
and was not able to finish.'"

Ridicule is a form of humor. Not a nice one. But a form nonetheless. Like the reaction people give to my new haircut: "I've seen worse. In fact, I don't think it's nearly as bad as everyone else says." To which I say: "Thank you?"

You Know You're Hungry When You …
Ponder Pig Pods
(A.k.a. The Prominent Problems
of Prodigality)

Luke 15:11-16
Jesus tells the woeful tale of a man who demands his inheritance early and travels to a foreign land where his wealth runs out; and he's forced to feed pigs. He gets so hungry, he considers eating the pods that he feeds to the pigs!

One of the primary rules of standup comedy is: Know your audience. Here, Jesus demonstrates how well He does. What's the best way to gross out a Jewish audience? Have the hero of the story work with pigs. And give him an unhealthy hankering for Purina Pig Chow.

For a Fantastically Fun and Funny telling of the Parable of the Prodigal Son, listen to Track 2 "Parable in F" on Christian comedian Justin N. Fennell's CD "Just Clean Fun". And for more info about him and his comedy, visit his website at: www.JustCleanFun.com

Second Shortest?

Luke 17:32 (KJV):
Remember Lot's wife!

I'm guessing, but this may be the second shortest verse in the Bible. (With the shortest being John 11:35: "Jesus wept.") But is that verse funny? It's all in the delivery. It's all in how you say it. Try a goofy voice or some silly accent. Wear a funny hat! If you practice, I'm sure you'll find a funny way to say that. If not, wait until you're overtired or in a giddy mood; and try again. "Remember Lot's wife!" See?

Not Resistant to the Persistent

Luke 18:1-8
To encourage His disciples to pray and not lose heart, Jesus tells them a parable about a persistent widow who convinces a godless judge to

help her. The KJV says Jesus told this parable to show that men should always pray and not faint. If He didn't want them to faint, He could've suggested avoiding overexertion and drinking lots of fluids. At the very least, sit down once in a while and enjoy a good ceiling fan.

**While praying,
we suddenly felt the need to face a crisis.**

A Mina Infraction

Luke 19:11-27

Jesus tells the parable of the minas (an amount of money worth about three months' wages). Instead of "doing business" as his master commanded, the wicked servant hid his mina. In 19:20 (NASB): "And another came, saying, 'Master, here is your mina, which I have kept put away in a handkerchief.'"

That's a lot funnier in the original Aramaic. Especially if the guy speaking Aramaic has a funny accent. The joke is that the word for *handkerchief* means *sweat rag*. Instead of working and using the sweat rag to wipe his brow, the lazy servant was so lazy. (How lazy was he?) He was so lazy, he buried his sweat rag in the ground with his mina, his talent. Two thousand years later; that joke's not as funny any more, but back then, the disciples used to gather around the fire on cool Galilean nights and beg Jesus, "Master please, tell us the one about the lazy servant. That one's a riot."

**How many Messiahs does it take
to change a light bulb?
… One,
because there is only one.**

We've Got a Winner!

Luke 19:23 (NASB):
"Why then did you not put my money in the bank,
that at my coming
I might have collected it with interest?"

An ideal Win!-Win!-Win! Situation: The bank gets a new customer; the man of noble birth receives his mina back plus interest; and the servant gets a free toaster for opening a new account.

**How many Sons of God does it take
to change a light bulb?
… None,
because Jesus shines in glory
and doesn't need a light bulb.**

What's Cooking?

Luke 24:41 (NIV):
And while they [the disciples] still did not believe it
because of joy and amazement,
he [Jesus] asked them,
"Do you have anything here to eat?"

I wonder how many hungry teens realize how often they quote Jesus.

To wrap up the Synoptic Gospels, here's ...

Portrait of a Puppet Procurator: A.k.a. Auto-Pilate: The Reluctant Christ-Killer with a Penchant for Hygiene

Pontius Pilate had it tough. To begin with, procurator of Judea was not the dream job for Roman politicians. Akin to the Russian Front for Nazis in World War Two as recounted on "Hogan's Heroes". (Only without the risk of frostbite and hypothermia. And with no danger of being mauled by a rabid polar bear or an abominable yeti.)

Still, overseeing the Roman stronghold over Judea remained a step or two above decapitation, so Pilate had that going for him. But then again, one more major mistake; and heads would roll! Well, his would anyway. And I say "one more major mistake", because he must have done something reprehensible to be assigned such a joyless job. Or maybe he bought into the notion that such an assignment would be his stepping stone to a pristine appointment to the Roman Senate. Either way, with the past problems between Rome and Judea, Pilate presided in that precarious position of one more strike; and he's out. Thus, he'd do anything to avoid an all-out revolt. Who knows? Maybe he lied on his résumé and said he majored in quashing unwanted uprisings with the greatest of ease.

Having decided Jesus deserved to die, because they considered His claim to be God blasphemous; and because they envied His ability to draw such great adoring crowds, the Sanhedrin took Jesus to Pontius Pilate. Because Rome wouldn't allow the Judeans to execute their own people. The Romans couldn't let them have all the fun. Right?

And so, along comes Jesus. Introduced to Pilate one early Friday morning as a prophet from Nazareth who stirs up the people. And yet, He displayed Himself as a meek, yet mighty, man. And, as possibly, much more than a mere man. Why wasn't He belligerent and defiant like all the other prisoners brought before him?

To make matters worse, as if they could get any worse, Pilate's wife sends him a note telling him to have nothing to do with this Righteous Man, because she suffered much in a dream about Him. So Pilate not only has to maintain peace between Rome and Judea, he must also keep his marriage in good straits too. If Mrs. Pilate's not happy; Pontius won't be either.

Pilate recognizes right away that the Sanhedrin turned Jesus over to him because of envy. Perhaps their potluck suppers and bingo nights failed to draw the numbers they used to. The Sanhedrin persist in accusing Jesus of all kinds of crimes. Meanwhile, Jesus keeps quiet. Which frustrates Pilate to no end. He doesn't want to execute an innocent man. If only to keep his wife happy! But it's so hard to prove someone's not guilty when that person refuses to defend himself.

On and on they accuse Jesus of sedition, forbidding people to pay taxes, and of defying Rome by claiming to be the Messiah, a king! Wow! What's a Roman procurator to do?

A lucky break comes when the Sanhedrin mentions that Jesus came from Galilee. Sweet! Thinks Pilate. He can dump the fatal decision into Herod's lap. Pilate had been excessively cruel to the Galileans, but after sending Jesus to Herod, Pilate and Herod become pals. Well, whatever kind of buddies vicious Roman rulers can become. Herod hopes to see a miracle and feels cheated when he doesn't. So his soldiers mock and beat Jesus, arraying Him in a royal robe. Too bad for Pilate, Herod stamps Jesus: "Return to Sender!" Poor Herod, had he hung around three more days, he would have seen The Greatest Miracle of All.

Pilate can't get rid of Jesus. Not conveniently anyway. Like a well-thrown boomerang, He keeps coming back. Or like relatives and in-laws when they hear you won the lottery, He just won't go away. Pilate ponders profusely. Wait a minute, isn't this the Passover? Since Pilate couldn't pass off Jesus to Herod, perhaps he could "Pass Over" Him. He announces he will uphold his previous tradition of releasing one prisoner for the Feast of Passover. He points to Jesus, nods like a bobblehead in an earthquake, and asks, "How about Him?" Unfortunately, the Sanhedrin chooses Barabbas. Yes, the Barabbas, who committed murder in sedition against Rome. Presumably, he killed Roman soldiers; tantamount to being a Cop-Killer today. Not the guy you want to release if you hope to court favor with Rome.

So far, he's made friends with Herod and rid the Roman prison of an annoying enemy without bothering to execute him. And to top things off, he still has this so-called King of the Jews on his hands. To be polite, and to show how "fair" he can be, Pilate orders Jesus to be flogged. But how does that make sense, if Pilate claims He's innocent? "To placate you, I shall violently beat and torture this Innocent Man." Pilate's already run out of sensible options, so that's the best he can come up with. He thinks seeing Jesus mutilated will satiate their thirst for blood. But then again, he also thought wearing a laurel on his head looked stately.

Maybe if he picked off the aphids first.

"Behold the Man!"

"Behold your King!"

Oops! Wrong thing to say, 'cause suddenly, the members of the Sanhedrin become the biggest fans of Rome. "We have no king but Caesar!" They also mention how Pilate's making himself an enemy of Rome by not executing Jesus. Oh-oh. Pilate doesn't want that. Nothing kills a career quicker than making one's self an enemy of his employer.

That's bad enough. Isn't it? From a secular point-of-view anyway. But then the Sanhedrin mentions that Jesus claims to be the Son of God. Oh boy! Now Pilate must worry about offending the Divine too! As if Rome, his wife, and the Sanhedrin weren't enough!

Pilate questions Jesus.   Jesus doesn't answer. Pilate throws a hissy fit. Here he tries to find a way to release Jesus; and Jesus won't help him. "Are You not going to answer me?! Don't You know I have the authority to crucify You? Or to release You?" Jesus knows. He tells him he wouldn't have any authority if it hadn't been given from above.

The Sanhedrin resume their chorus of "If you let Him go, Caesar won't invite you to his parties." And, of course, "Crucify Him! Crucify Him!"

Pilate washes his hands, but his is a stain not easily washed away.   Not with soap and water anyway.   He surrenders Jesus to their will and orders Him crucified.

And, as if to show he still has the final say, he writes on the sign which declares the "crime" for which Jesus is being crucified: "Jesus of Nazareth, The King of the Jews".

Funny thing is, the way the sign would have been written in Hebrew, the four main letters would have been JHVH. Yes, that's the Hebrew name for God. Inadvertently, Pilate placed a sign over Jesus' head declaring Him to be the God of the Jews, not just the King. That's why the chief priests become so upset. They wanted to rid themselves of the Prophet from Nazareth, not deify Him. To which, Pilate replies, "What I have written, I have written."

Poor Pilate, he probably slept on the couch that night.   And maybe for a long time thereafter. One tradition claims he went mad and languished in an asylum where he continually washed his hands. But like I said, his was a stain not easily washed away. But that's true for all of us. Until Jesus washes us clean.

Poor Pontius, he was a Pilate who crashed and burned.

JOHN

Matthew just means "Gift of God", but John means "Gracious Gift of God". Perhaps that's one of the perks of being the Beloved Disciple. Funny thing is, no one else refers to John that way. Hmm. And he waited until after all the other disciples had been killed to write that. I'm just saying ...

To Be Said Sarcastically ...

John 1:46b (RSV):
"Can anything good come out of Nazareth?"

The Message Bible presents that same line as: "Nazareth? You've got to be kidding."

Watch Out for Falling Figs

John 1:47-51
When Jesus tells Nathanael He saw him sitting under the fig tree, Nathanael replies, "Rabbi, You are the Son of God! The King of Israel!" Jesus says, "Because I said to you, 'I saw you under the fig tree,' do you believe?" He tells him he'll see even greater things than these!

Thomas needed lots of convincing to believe Jesus is the Son of God. But not Nathanael. Jesus says He saw him sitting under a fig tree; and Nathanael boldly proclaims Christ's divinity!

Some folks readily believe the sign that says "Wet Paint"; while others must touch.

Jesus turning water into wine was great,
but I wish He'd change bricks into chocolate.
Some homes would double in value overnight;
then plummet the next day,
after all the neighbors stop by for a bite.

Nicodemus Can Be So Brave
... Under Cover of Darkness

John 3:1-4

Slick Nick boldly comes to Jesus at night! He doesn't want his buddies at the Pharisees Club making fun of him for being the Messiah's pet.

We must be born again?! Fortunately, for mothers everywhere, Jesus already suffered the pangs needed for us to be reborn.

Nick's response to Jesus' saying we must be born again: "How can a man be born when he is old? Can he enter the second time into his mother's womb, and be born?" Ouch! Let's hope not. I think that'd be painful for everyone involved. Even the obstetrician.

Live for Christ with joy and enthusiasm!
We're called to be born again; not bored again.

No One Wants to Get that Kind of Stoned

John 8:2-12

The Pharisees bring a woman caught in adultery to Jesus. They say Moses commanded that she should be stoned. Then they ask Him, "But what do You say?" In John 8:7 (NCV) Jesus says: "Anyone here who has never sinned can throw the first stone at her."

Who was the Only One there Who never sinned? Hmm? Was Jesus merely making the point that we shouldn't judge, 'cause we all have sin in our lives, or did He want to be the One to throw the first stone? (I know the Real Answer; it's just a joke. Okay? Before you start picking up stones, reread that passage several times.)

The expressions on the Pharisees' faces must've been funny. As each one realized his own sin, he reluctantly dropped the stone he had hoped to throw and sulked away. They thought they had trapped Jesus. No matter which way He answered, A or B, He'd be in trouble. But Jesus came up with Answer C and stymied them. And then they sulked away like the General Mills' Rabbit when he's refused a bowl of Trix. Silly Pharisees!

I Always Try to Tell the Truth, 'Cause Lies Are Too Hard to Remember!

John 8:32 (RSV):
"and you will know the truth,
and the truth will make you free."

When I first visited my church, I told the Pastor: "I want a church that's not afraid to proclaim the truth."

And lo, he didst say unto me, "Your outfit doesn't match; your haircut's funny; and you walk like a duck."

I said, "Thank you robustly for your candor." But not in those exact words.

We Be Free

John 8:33 (NIV):
They [the Jews who had believed Jesus]
answered him [Jesus],
"We are Abraham's descendants
and have never been slaves of anyone.
How can you say that we shall be set free?"

Did these Jewish believers not read where Egypt enslaved Abraham's descendants? How could they not? That fact is foundational to their faith! What was the point of the Passover if they weren't freed from slavery? That's like dairy farmers in the Alps saying, "We are Swiss and have never made hole-ly cheese."

The Serpent Speaks with a Forked Tongue and Usually Says: "Sssssssssssss!"

John 8:44c (NIV):
"When he [the Devil] lies,
he speaks his native language,
for he is a liar and the father of lies."

<u>Funny joke by Jesus</u>: Lying is the Devil's native language!

We Wanna Talk to You about Your Kid

John 9:18-22

The Pharisees don't believe that the healed blind man had been blind, so they question his parents. Mom and Pop deftly avoid being banned from the synagogue by saying that yes, he's their son, but regarding the details surrounding his miraculous healing, they'll have to ask him, because he's old enough to speak for himself.

No need to get the whole family in trouble when Junior can take the fall by himself. Right?

"'I See,' Said the Blind Man As He Picked Up His Hammer and Saw"*

* Traditional nonsense verse.

John 9:26-27 (RSV):
They [the Pharisees] said
to him [the man who had been blind],
"What did he do to you?
How did he open your eyes?"
He answered them, "I have told you already,
and you would not listen.
Why do you want to hear it again?
Do you too want to become his disciples?"

Asking Pharisees if they want to be disciples of Jesus is like asking carnivores if they want to be vegans. "I already told you how I made the salad, but you wouldn't listen. Why do you keep asking me? Do you too want to become vegans?" "Roar!"

What a Bunch of Stoners!

John 10:30-33 (NIV):
[Jesus said to the Pharisees,]
"I and the Father are one."
Again the Jews picked up stones to stone him,
but Jesus said to them, "I have shown you
many great miracles from the Father.
For which of these do you stone me?"
"We are not stoning you for any of these,"
replied the Jews, "but for blasphemy,
because you, a mere man, claim to be God."

Jesus knows why they want to stone Him. Perhaps He asks this question so no one can say He never claimed to be God. Nor can they say He doesn't have a sense of humor. As if the "Lying is the Devil's language" joke wasn't proof enough.

The Apostle Peter's All Washed Up (Except for His Feet)

John 13:1-17
Jesus, the Lord and Master for His disciples for the last three to three and a half years, sets aside his robe, drapes a towel around Himself like a servant, and washes His disciples' feet. Peter protests, seemingly offended His Lord would stoop

so low. He forbids Jesus to wash His feet. (Who knows? Maybe he had a funny-shaped second toe. Many of us do. Acclaimed scholars never fully broach that subject.) Jesus tells Peter that unless He washes him, he won't have any part with Him. Peter doesn't want to lose his Disciple Membership Card, so he tells Jesus to wash his hands and head too. Jesus says those who have cleaned themselves need only have their feet washed. Peter acquiesces. Jesus talks about how He gave us an example and that we should wash one another's feet.

Poor Peter, situations twist around so quickly for him. He steps out of the boat to walk on water, but noticing the boisterous waves, he begins to sink. He declares Jesus is the Son of God, but seconds later, says he won't let Him be crucified, earning the harshest of admonitions: "Get behind me, Satan!" And when he warms himself at a fire, a servant girl identifies him as a disciple of Jesus. A fact Peter denies three times with increasing intensity, even though he previously promised Jesus he'd die with Him. And yet, hearing Jesus is no longer in the grave, he races to the tomb. Not as fast as John, but as fast as he can go.

You can see where Peter got some of his wrong ideas: In Luke 17:4 Jesus says that if someone wrongs you seven times in one day and turns to you seven times to ask for forgiveness, you must forgive that person all seven times. In Matthew 18:21, when Peter asks Jesus if he must forgive his brother seven times, he might be showing off how well he listens. Until the next verse, where Jesus says for him to forgive, not seven times, but seventy times seven. In the aforementioned foot-washing incident, if having his feet washed by Jesus makes him a part of God's kingdom, why stop with the feet? Throw in the hands and head too! And in Luke 22, Jesus tells His disciples to buy a sword. When they say they have two. Jesus says, "It is enough." So when the soldiers arrest Jesus in the Garden of Gethsemane, what does Peter do? He strikes with his sword and cuts off Malchus' ear. Only to be reprimanded again.

Still, Peter's the only disciple to walk on water. He meant well when he offered to build tents for Moses, Elijah, and Jesus. And when asked to acknowledge Who Jesus Is, he nailed it, declaring Jesus is the Christ, the Son of the Living God; and he recognized that He has the words of eternal life. At some point in our lives, we've probably all denied Jesus a lot more than three times. And if our mistakes were written in a book, we'd make Peter look like a saint.

**When fighting temptation,
put your soul at cross-purposes
with the Devil's schemes.**

**My favorite Christmas carol:
"Happy Birthday Jesus;
The One Who Set Us Free;
You're Centuries Old;
But Still Look Thirty-Three"**

"The Last Sopper"

John 13:26

I'm appalled that criminals on death row enjoy more sumptuous last meals than our loving Lord did. Serial killers, rapists, and traitors alike enjoy elaborate meals, but based on the so-called "Holy Communion" offered at some churches, you'd think Jesus went to face His demise after only a smattering of juice and crackers.

As far as last meals go, would Belgian waffles with fresh strawberries and whipped cream be asking too much?

What about a peanut butter and banana sandwich? On whole-grain bread, of course. Have to have a healthy diet. Unless there's chocolate involved. And then we can fudge.

But then again, if it's our last meal anyway, why not gorge on ice cream and pie? With lots of whipped cream and hot fudge sauce!

In John 13:26, Jesus tells John that His betrayer is the one to whom Jesus hands the bread after He dips it. (The KJV says "sop" instead of bread, so does that make this The Last Sopper?)

When Jesus instituted The Lord's Supper, He used unleavened bread, not leavened bread, not stale crackers, and definitely not packing chips. And He used red wine, not white grape juice, not purple Gatorade, and definitely not Grape Koolaid!

Ritz Crackers and Goofy Grape do not a Sacrament make!

Do You Suffer from P. P. S.?

John 18:38 (NIV):
"What is truth?" Pilate asked.
With this he went out again to the Jews and said,
"I find no basis for a charge against him.
&
Matthew 27:24 (NIV):
When Pilate saw that he was getting nowhere,
but that instead an uproar was starting,
he took water
and washed his hands in front of the crowd.
"I am innocent of this man's blood," he said.
"It is your responsibility!"

If you ever wonder what is Truth; and afterwards want to wash your hands, that's Pontius Pilate Syndrome.

And if, after all that, you want to fly a plane, that's Pontius Pilot Syndrome.

And if one or both of your lower extremities quakes erratically, that's Restless Leg Syndrome.

Peter Came In
Second To Last

John 20:3-8
John goes to great lengths to emphasize that he outran Peter to the tomb. Why? Does the winner get to sit next to Jesus in Heaven?

'Cause I know how important that is to John and his mom.

The Latest in Galilean Swimwear

John 21:7 (The Message):
Then the disciple Jesus loved said to Peter,
"It's the Master!"
When Simon Peter realized that it was the Master,
he threw on some clothes,
for he was stripped for work,
and dove into the sea.

He puts on his clothes to dive into the sea. Seems the opposite of what you'd expect. Unless you're putting on a swimsuit, wouldn't you take off your clothes to go swimming? I know it's not like he rented a tux to go for a morning dip. But still.

<u>ACTS</u>
(a.k.a. The Acts of the Apostles)

Perhaps the title should be "The Acts of the Holy Spirit Performed Through the Apostles". As the Holy Spirit helps to chop away sin's hold on our lives, we could call this the book of Ax.

**When you fan the flames of faith,
you can catch Satan in the crossfire.**

Comes with a Son Roof!

Acts 2:1 (KJV):
And when the day of Pentecost was fully come,
they were all with one accord in one place.

I purposefully avoided old Bible jokes in this book. Like the baseball one which refers to the opening of the Bible as "In the Big Inning". Or the silly one asking about the circus bear in the Bible: "Gladly, the Cross-Eyed Bear". I'm usually not a big fan of such hokey humor. 'Cause it's so horrid. And reprehensible. Unless I write it!

So here we go ... What kind of car did the disciples drive? ... A Honda. Because the Bible says they were all in one Accord.

That kind of joke can use an adept drummer pounding out a rim shot. Where's Ringo when we need him?

Don't drive badly. Ever.
But especially if you have
a "Honk If You Love Jesus"
bumper sticker on your car.
'Cause that reflects poorly on Christians.
And don't kid yourself into thinking
everyone who honks at you loves Jesus.
Even if the honker shouts His name.

What Have You Been Drinking?

Acts 2:13 (The Message):
Others joked, "They're drunk on cheap wine."

A classic insult, still in use today. Although nowadays, at some senior centers and nursing homes, it's sometimes rephrased as: "Someone's had too much Geritol."

An Angel Busts Peter
Out of the Big House

Acts 12:1-19a

The Angel awakens Peter with a "smote" to his side and tells him to get up, get dressed, and follow him! Peter obeys, but thinks he's dreaming. The Angel leads Peter past the first and second guards; and the iron gate opens by itself. After walking a block or so, the Angel disappears. Realizing the Lord sent an angel to set him free, he hurries to the house of Mary the mother of John Mark and says, "Can you take dictation? I've got a great idea for a gospel!" Okay, maybe he didn't say that. At least not right away.

Peter knocks on the door; and Rhoda, a damsel not in distress, comes to the door. Hearing his voice, she's so happy she runs back to tell the others without opening the door. She says Peter's at the door. Since Herod imprisoned him after killing James, they think there's no way Peter got a Get Out of Jail Free card. So they politely inform Rhoda that she's gone mad. She keeps saying he's at the door. But they say it must be his angel or his ghost. Meanwhile, Peter keeps knocking!

Finally, they open the door; and Peter explains what happened. The next morning at Herod's prison, as Luke says with a bit of wry understatement: There's "no small disturbance". Like the 1960 Valdivia Earthquake with a whopping record 9.5 on the Richter scale caused no small stir.

Herod's Bad Day
(His Last One Alive)

Acts 12:19b-23

Arrayed in royal apparel, more than a T-shirt and tattered jeans, Herod gives a speech to the people of Tyre and Sidon. (I think they were just the people of Sidon, but the speech lasted so long, they became Tyred as well.) The people shout that he speaks with the voice of a god, not a man. So Herod thinks he's doing great. When really, they're just sucking up, 'cause their country gets food from his country. Since Herod takes upon himself the adulation that belongs to God, an angel smites him. And thus, Herod's eaten by worms and dies. (Obviously, the angel smote Herod harder than he smote Peter. Takes less smiting to awaken someone than to strike them dead.) Notice how Herod gets it backwards too. Most people die; and then get eaten by worms. But he gets eaten by worms and then dies. Silly Herod, praise is for God.

My Undercover Alias
Is Bean Turkey

Acts 13:9

Saul is also called Paul. What?! If you want to change your name, so people won't think of you as that horrid person who dragged off believers to prison and the gallows, don't change it to something so similar to your real name that people confuse the two. That'd be like Hitler repenting of his evil ways and wanting to help the Jews, but to ensure they'll trust him, he changes his name to Bitler.

In his case, it might've helped if he also shaved off his Charlie Chaplin mustache.

And stopped hanging around Bussolini.

**Name-calling
is for losers.**

Barnabas and Paul Win "Lystra Idol"

Acts 14:8-18

Paul heals a crippled man in Lystra by telling him to stand on his feet. So the town goes crazy and declares that the gods have come down in the likeness of men. They call Paul Hermes, because he does most of the talking, which, by default, leaves Barnabas as Zeus, the chief of their gods. (<u>Helpful Hint</u>: If you want people to think you're more important than you are, don't talk so much.) The crowd tries to offer sacrifices to them, but Barnabas and Paul tear their clothes, chide them for being so superstitious, and segue into declaring the Gospel. Even then, they have trouble keeping the people from sacrificing to them. Seems sad, you help someone, but wind up with your clothes torn.

And the fun's not over yet folks, soon thereafter, some Jews from Antioch and Iconium arrive and convince the crowd to stone Paul to death. Yes, the same crowd that declared Paul to be a god stones him to death! Or so they think. After they leave Paul's body outside the city, the disciples huddle around him; and he rises up. But before leaving, he goes back into the city! Why? So he could chant?: "You missed me! You missed me! Now you've gotta kiss me!"

Paul and Silas in the Big House (No, Not a Large Dwelling, The Slammer! The Pokey! Okay, Prison)

Acts 16:16-40

A slave girl with a fortune-telling spirit follows Paul and his entourage around, declaring that they are men of God who proclaim the way of Salvation. You'd think positive publicity would be a good thing. But after a few days, Paul gets annoyed and casts the spirit out of her. Naturally, the folks in the fortune-telling biz feel dismayed to see their moneymaker lose her precognitive powers. So they drag Paul and Silas to court. The crowd joins in. The magistrates flog Paul and Silas, fling them into prison, and fasten their feet in stocks.

You'd think those guy's be tuckered out after such a long day, but nope. Come midnight, those two are still awake. Grumbling about their tough times? Nope. Praying and singing praises to God! So loudly, they keep the other prisoners awake. But they wouldn't have slept long anyway, since soon thereafter, an earthquake judders the jail, damages the doors, and shakes off their shackles.

The jailer awakens and figures he'll be fired, 'cause he thinks everyone's skedaddled. Not wanting to go to the unemployment office, he draws his sword to filet his innards. But Paul calls out, telling him not to hurt himself, 'cause everyone's still there. Overjoyed he doesn't have to slice and dice his insides, the jailer asks Paul and Silas how he can be saved.

Meanwhile, the magistrates send messengers telling the jailer that Paul and Silas are free to go. All's well that ends well; right? Nope. Paul isn't satisfied with just being set free. He tells the officers that they beat and threw good Roman citizens in prison without a trial, so they'd better not expect them to leave quietly. They'd better come and release them themselves. "Wait a minute. You guys are Roman citizens?! Oh-oh!"

So they come, being much more cordial than the day before. "We didn't mean nothin' by it. Just go. Please!" And so they leave. Paul gets good mileage out of his Roman citizenship. But you'd think he'd've mentioned that <u>before</u> the beating.

Sky-Side Up

Acts 17:6 (ESV):
And when they could not find them,
they dragged Jason and some of the brothers
before the city authorities, shouting, "These men
who have turned the world upside down
have come here also,

If only we'd be so bold as to turn the world upside down. Which, in the case of our world, would be setting it right side up.

What?!
I'm the only one in the whole church
to whom Pastor gave
missionary brochures to Antarctica?

I'd Love to Help You,
Except that I Don't Want To

Acts 18:14-15 (NASB):
But when Paul was about to open his mouth,
Gallio said to the Jews,
"If it were a matter of wrong or of vicious crime,
O Jews,
it would be reasonable
for me to put up with you;
but if there are questions
about words and names and your own law,
look after it yourselves;
I am unwilling to be a judge of these matters."

Way to go, Gallio! Best way to avoid a
fight, is not to get involved. Plus, he knew not to let
Paul start talking or they'd never get out of there
before closing time.

A Little Help Please!

Acts 18:17
While the Greeks beat Sosthenes, Gallio
ignores them. Pays them no mind whatsoever.
Imagine him trying to carry on a conversation with
the sounds of Sosthenes getting beaten in the

background. "Have you seen the latest chariot?" Ouch! "Yes, I like the new design for the front. Makes running over enemy soldiers so much easier." Ow!! "Indeed, artistic, yet practical." Yee-Owww!!! "I think we're due for some rain."

Exorcise at Least Three Times a Week (A.k.a. The Seven Sons of Sceva Suffer So)

Acts 19:13-16 (The Message)
Some itinerant Jewish exorcists
who happened to be in town at the time
tried their hand
at what they assumed to be Paul's "game."
They pronounced the name of the Master Jesus
over victims of evil spirits, saying,
"I command you by the Jesus preached by Paul!"
The seven sons of a certain Sceva,
a Jewish high priest, were trying to do this
on a man when the evil spirit talked back:
"I know Jesus and I've heard of Paul,
but who are you?"
Then the possessed man went berserk
—jumped the exorcists,
beat them up, and tore off their clothes.
Naked and bloody, they got away as best they could.

Fleeing naked causes further complications that can get you in the end, so before you attempt to cast out evil spirits, apply SPF 45.

When Long Sermons Turn Deadly

Acts 20:7-12

Poor Eutychus. He sits in a window listening to Paul preach well past midnight. Not long thereafter, the young man not only falls asleep, but falls out the window. To his death! <u>The Pastoral Point is clear</u>: Long-windedness can kill!

Getting to the point of one's sermon quicker saves lives! On the plus side, Paul brings him back to life. But then he continues preaching until daybreak. Some preachers never learn. Make your point. Pass around the plate. Pray. Sing a song or two. And then send us into the world to fulfill the Great Commission. Or visit an all-you-can-eat buffet. Whichever comes first. When you talk too long, we won't be able to hear you over our hungry stomachs. Growl!

<u>Helpful Hint</u>:
Hug your pastor;
and he may preach faster.

Do As I Say,
Not As I Don't Say

Acts 21:22-23a (NIV):
"What shall we do?
They will certainly hear that you have come,
so do what we tell you."

What shall we do? We'll tell you what to do!

Born to Roam; I'm a Roamin' Guy!

Acts 22:21-29

After Paul tells a crowd of Jewish believers the Lord's sending him to the Gentiles, they shout Paul should be removed from the Earth; he isn't fit to live. To add to the fun, they cast off their cloaks and fling dust in the air.

Paul guesses the Secret Word. Gentiles! Say that to a crowd in ancient Jerusalem; and you're sure to start a fervor. The commander orders Paul taken into the barracks to be flogged and questioned to determine why the crowd reacted so harshly. As the soldiers prepare Paul for a hearty flogging, he slyly asks, "Is it legal to flog a Roman citizen before he's tried and found guilty?" Yay! This time he mentions his citizenship <u>before</u> being beaten.

The commander says he bought his citizenship for a lot of money. Paul replies, "But I was born a citizen." Being born a citizen trumps a purchased citizenship. The soldiers withdraw from flogging Paul. And the commander grows gravely concerned he put an uncondemned Roman in chains. Oops! Not the sort of thing a Roman commander wants on his résumé. Do that too often; and Caesar might demote you to lion-feeder.

**According to most televangelists today,
the way of Salvation seems to be:**

Repent, Believe, and Donate.

Not necessarily in that order.

How to Divide a Divisive Crowd

Acts 23:1-9

Paul calls the Sanhedrin his brothers and declares he has served God in good conscience. Not convinced, the high priest Ananias orders those nearby to strike Paul on the mouth.

Paul chastises Ananias, "God will strike you, you whitewashed wall! You sit to judge me according to the law, but you break the law by ordering me to be struck?" Maybe "whitewashed wall" was the big insult back then. Much like "Chicken Lips" is today. Or "Turkey Toes". (People can be so cruel.) Because those nearby chide Paul for insulting the high priest. To which Paul replies, "My bad!" Or something like that.

Determining the assembly is half Pharisees and half Sadducees, Paul declares he is a Pharisee and the son of a Pharisee and stands trial because of his hope in the Resurrection. The council becomes divided. Not only are the Pharisees pro-Pharisee; they're also pro-resurrection, pro-angel, and pro-spirit. Whereas the Sadducees are anti all that.

Suddenly, the Pharisees argue on behalf of Paul's innocence, saying "So what if a spirit or angel spoke to him? Who are we to fight against God?" Those who had wanted him killed now wish him well. Nowadays, one might achieve the same effect by yelling "Crunchy wheat!"* since the half the crowd will shout back "Nicely sweet!"*

* Lines from, and a reference to, past commercials for Kellogg's Frosted Mini-Wheats.

Can We Finish This
Before Lunch?
I'm Gettin' Kinda Hungry

Acts 23:13-14

More than forty conspirators take a solemn oath not to eat or drink anything until after they kill Paul. But they never get to kill Paul. So eventually, to avoid starving to death or dying of thirst, they must rationalize: "When we say we took a solemn oath, what do we really mean by solemn? I think it means, hey, we took a shot, but things didn't work out, so let's all enjoy an all-you-can-eat buffet. We just won't eat Brussels sprouts. Yeah, that's what our oath is: No more Brussels sprouts."

Ah yes, rationalization is a sweet defense mechanism. And so are Rocky Road and Mint Chocolate Chip.

Oo! Oo!
Look at Me! Look at Me!
I'm a Hero!

Acts 23:26-30

The commander writes to Governor Felix and makes himself appear much more noble and heroic than what really happened. He claims he rescued Paul, 'cause he learned he was a Roman citizen. More like he was going to flog Paul till he learned he was a Roman citizen. There's reality; and then there's the commander's fanciful version.

The Honorable (?) Felix Presiding

Acts 24:1-27

Both Tertullus and Paul suck up to Felix in their opening statements. In the KJV, Tertullus refers to Paul as a "pestilent".

Felix claims he'll decide the case when Lysias the commander arrives, but instead, he leaves Paul in prison for two years, all the while hoping Paul will offer him a bribe.

Pestilent isn't a compliment. And that's just what they could print in the Bible.

Don't Let Festus Arrest Us!

Acts 25:12 (NASB):
Then when Festus had conferred with his council,
he answered,
"You have appealed to Caesar,
to Caesar you shall go."

In "The Alleluia Follies," the musical version of the Book of Acts, this is where the whole cast bursts out singing: "To Caesar you shall go, to Caesar you shall go, heigh-ho, the derry-o, to Caesar you shall go."

How Absurd!

Acts 25:27 (NASB):
"For it seems absurd to me in sending a prisoner,
not to indicate also the charges against him."

Hail, Caesar! How's world domination going? I'm sending you this prisoner Paul, but I have no inkling why. I don't know what he did wrong. I don't even know his last name! Hope that won't affect my career adversely. Anyhoo, if you still need a gift idea for Brutus, I think he mentioned a fondness for cutlery.

I'm Beggin' You!

Acts 26:2-3 (NASB):
"In regard to all the things
of which I am accused by the Jews,
I consider myself fortunate, King Agrippa,
that I am about to make my defense before you
today; especially because you are an expert
in all customs and questions among the Jews;
therefore I beg you to listen to me patiently."

Paul's reputation as a Lonnnnnnnggggggg Talker requires him to beg to be heard! Patiently.

Shackled & Tackled

Acts 26:24-29 (NCV):
While Paul was saying these things
to defend himself,
Festus said loudly, "Paul, you are out of your mind!
Too much study has driven you crazy!"
Paul said, "Most excellent Festus, I am not crazy.
My words are true and sensible.
King Agrippa knows about these things,

and I can speak freely to him.
I know he has heard about all of these things,
because they did not happen off in a corner.
King Agrippa,
do you believe what the prophets wrote?
I know you believe."
King Agrippa said to Paul,
"Do you think you can persuade me
to become a Christian in such a short time?"
Paul said, "Whether it is a short or a long time,
I pray to God that not only you
but every person listening to me today
would be saved and be like me
—except for these chains I have."

The Notorious Northeaster!

Acts 27:14 (NCV):
But then a very strong wind
named the "northeaster" came from the island.

The KJV calls it "Euroclydon", but I like the name "northeaster". Makes me think of an old farmer with a long piece of straw dangling from his mouth as he drawls, "Yep, we almost lost the farm a while back, but I boarded up the barn to protect the herd from The Northeaster." He then spits chewing tobacco on your shoes; and you wonder why you bothered getting out of your car in such a place.

What's the best way to look at your soul?
… Cross examination.

ROMANS

Romans means more than one man who rows. As in, "This isn't my canoe; it's the Romans."

The Greeks Are Wise; But You Non-Greeks, Not So Much

Romans 1:14-15 (NASB):
I am under obligation
both to Greeks and to barbarians,
both to the wise and to the foolish.
So, for my part, I am eager to preach the gospel
to you also who are in Rome.

Did he insult his intended readers in Rome? The Romans aren't Greeks; and the non-Greeks are listed second. Thus, the Greeks are wise, but the barbarians, a.k.a. the Romans, are not!

How Can They Be Any Worse?

Romans 1:30 (NASB):
slanderers, haters of God, insolent, arrogant,
boastful, inventors of evil, disobedient to parents,

That's all kinds of naughty right there. They're so evil, they invent evil!

But then again, "inventors of evil" might refer to the inventors who came up with speed bumps, artificial sugar, and the Singing Bass.

1 CORINTHIANS

Corinth means "Which Is Satisfied, Ornament, Beauty". So Corinthian means "Which-Is-Satisfiedian, Ornamentian, Beautyian".

"Why Can't We All Just Get Along?"*

Line from the 1996 movie "Mars Attacks".

1 Corinthians 1:10-16 (NIV):
I appeal to you, brothers,
in the name of our Lord Jesus Christ,
that all of you agree with one another
so that there may be no divisions among you
and that you may be perfectly united
in mind and thought. My brothers,
some from Chloe's household have informed me
that there are quarrels among you.
What I mean is this:
One of you says, "I follow Paul";
another, "I follow Apollos";
another, "I follow Cephas [Peter]";
still another, "I follow Christ."
Is Christ divided? Was Paul crucified for you?
Were you baptized into the name of Paul?
I am thankful that I did not baptize any of you
except Crispus and Gaius, so no one can say
that you were baptized into my name.
(Yes, I also baptized the household of Stephanas;
beyond that,
I don't remember if I baptized anyone else.)

<u>To those from Chloe's household</u>: No one likes a snitch! (Especially the snitchees!) "Chloe's the Apostle's pet! Chloe's the Apostle's pet!"

Paul refers to himself in the third person. Like in "The Jimmy" episode of "Seinfeld" where a guy named Jimmy refers to himself in the third person: "Oh yeah! Jimmy couldn't jump at all before he got these. Jimmy was like you." "Jimmy likes Elaine." An odd idiosyncrasy which George adopts: "George is getting angry!"

Paul asks if he was crucified for the Corinthians. Was anyone whose name they wore like a banner the Christ? Sadly, that reminds me of today. Calvinists, Lutherans, Wesleyans, etc. Was John Calvin crucified for you? Were you baptized into the name of John Calvin? Sure, he has the right initials, but that's not good enough.

How old was Paul at this time? Already he can't recall whom he has and hasn't baptized. Didn't they have Ginkgo biloba back then?

Whip It Good!*

A line from the 1980 song "Whip It" by the American New Wave band Devo.

1 Corinthians 4:21 (NIV):
What do you prefer?
Shall I come to you with a whip,
or in love and with a gentle spirit?

Is that a trick question?
Oddly, I think Devo would prefer the whip.

You Know?

1 Corinthians 8:2 (NIV):
The man who thinks he knows something
does not yet know as he ought to know.

For added fun, say that ten times fast. While
patting your head, rubbing your belly, and hopping
on one foot. On a high wire! Over a shark tank.
Have someone video. Even if you don't make the
news, you'll garner a slew of hits on YouTube.

Paul the Contortionist?!

1 Corinthians 9:27a (KJV):
But I [Paul] keep under my body,

If Paul keeps under his body, how does he
walk? That must be quite a trick. Does he find a lot
of lost change down there?

One Body,
Lots 'O Parts

1 Corinthians 12:14-20
Paul explains how each part of the body
plays an important part. He even mentions our
unmentionables! Well, he alludes to them anyway.
If he mentioned them, they wouldn't be
unmentionable; would they?
If the ear says, "I'm no eye, so I have no
place in the body", would it suddenly cease to be a
part of the body? If the whole body were an eye,

what would hold up our glasses? If our whole body were a nose, how would we spray air freshener? How could we hold our hankies when we sneeze? Without mouths, who would bless us when we do?

We've Got Signs for Everybody

1 Corinthians 14:22-25 (NASB):
So then tongues are for a sign,
not to those who believe but to unbelievers;
but prophecy is for a sign,
not to unbelievers but to those who believe.
Therefore if the whole church assembles together
and all speak in tongues,
and ungifted men or unbelievers enter,
will they not say that you are mad?
But if all prophesy,
and an unbeliever or an ungifted man enters,
he is convicted by all, he is called to account by all;
the secrets of his heart are disclosed;
and so he will fall on his face and worship God,
declaring that God is certainly among you.

Did the translators get this backwards? Seems to me tongues would be a sign to believers because they know what tongues mean. Whereas prophecy would be a sign for unbelievers, because they'd hear words of supernatural power and believe! Even Paul's explanation seems to support this. Hearing the people speak in tongues makes the unbelievers think the believers are crazy, but hearing them prophesy makes them realize the believers really know God. But either way, seeing the offering plate makes them run!

Whom? Her? Or Hymn?

1 Corinthians 14:26
Paul gives his recipe for orderly worship, which includes the singing of hymns.

Who likes old hymns? I love old hymns so much, I wrote some. In fact, I wrote plenty. But the choir director at my church is so jealous of my hymn-writing abilities, she never lets the church sing any of them. Not a one.

I wrote such great hymns as: "Sing Loud Your Praises to the Lord, We Have to Drown Out Someone's Snores", "If You Cannot Join the Heavenly Host, You'd Better Believe Your Soul Is Toast", and the sad, yet theologically correct, with a funky dance beat: "Salvation Was Won at the Cross, So Stop Whining; and Don't Forget to Floss".

How pathetic some people let their petty envy get in the way of creative expression.

"Ch-Ch-Changes"*

From the 1971 song "Changes" by David Bowie.

1 Corinthians 15:51b (KJV):
We shall not all sleep,
but we shall all be changed --

Victory Church in Lakeland, Florida displays that verse outside their infant nursery.

2 CORINTHIANS

"Corinthians" is the name of those ornate columns with the swirly things. Thus, 2 Corinthians means a pair of fancy schmancy columns.

Comfy?

2 Corinthians 1:3-7 (NIV) (**Emphasis** added):
"Praise be to the God and Father of our Lord Jesus Christ, the Father of compassion and the God of all **comfort**, who **comforts** us in all our troubles, so that we can **comfort** those in any trouble with the **comfort** we ourselves have received from God. For just as the sufferings of Christ flow over into our lives, so also through Christ our **comfort** overflows. If we are distressed, it is for your **comfort** and salvation; if we are **comforted**, it is for your **comfort**, which produces in you patient endurance of the same sufferings we suffer. And our hope for you is firm, because we know that just as you share in our sufferings, so also you share in our **comfort**."

I'm gonna guess the key word is: **Comfort**!

Crazy Talk

2 Corinthians 11:19 (The Message):
Since you sit there in the judgment seat
observing all these shenanigans,
you can afford to humor
an occasional fool who happens along.

How can you not love a Sacred Scripture that uses the word "shenanigans"?

Don't Repeat the Unrepeatable

2 Corinthians 12:4b (The Message):
There he heard the unspeakable spoken,
but was forbidden to tell what he heard.

If the unspeakable can be spoken, does that mean we can mention the unmentionables?

That's Just Super!

2 Corinthians 12:11 (NIV):
I have made a fool of myself, but you drove me to it.
I ought to have been commended by you,
for I am not in the least inferior
to the "super-apostles," even though I am nothing.

Super Apostles! With amazing apostle powers far beyond those of mere mortal men.*

* *My variation/spoof of a line from the 1952-1958 ABC TV show "The Adventures of Superman".*

GALATIANS

Galatia comes from the root word Gaul. Thus, Paul wrote to the Galatians wondering how they could have the gall to act the way they did. Or maybe the town was overrun by gulls.

I Can't Help But Wonder:
Does Paul Ever Feel Guilty
That People Rob Peter to Pay Him?

Galatians 2:11-21

Precious Peter, that great guy who says he'll die with Christ, but moments later denies knowing Him. Not once, not twice, but three times! He's in trouble again. This time with Paul! Peter gets cozy with the Gentiles, hanging out, having a good time, being a pal. But as soon as Jews from James arrive, Peter and other Jews who had been buddy-buddy with the Gentiles, back away. Even Barnabas, our little Son of Encouragement, gets caught up in the phoniness. So, in front of everyone else, Paul slams Peter for trying to put a yoke on the Gentiles even the Jews can't keep, emphasizing Jesus died to save us, not enslave us. Poor Peter. When he's right; he's right. But when he's wrong, he's oh so wrong.

EPHESIANS

Ephesus means "Desirable". And yet, if you tell an attractive woman, she looks "So Ephesus", she acts like she's been insulted.

The Lowest of the Low

Ephesians 3:8 (KJV):
Unto me,
who am less than the least of all saints,
is this grace given,

that I should preach among the Gentiles
the unsearchable riches of Christ;

Can't get much lower than less than the least.   Unless you're less than the least's little brother.   Or his pet hamster.   Or what covers the bottom of his cage.

A Coarse Is a Coarse, Of Course, Of Course* (But I Wouldn't Dare Joke about That)

* My variation on the theme song (written by Jay Livingston and Ray Evans) for the 1961-1966 CBS show "Mister Ed".

Ephesians 5:3-4 (NKJV):
But fornication and all uncleanness or covetousness,
let it not even be named among you,
as is fitting for saints;
neither filthiness, nor foolish talking,
nor coarse jesting,
which are not fitting, but rather giving of thanks.

Coarse jesting is wrong.   Any joke that starts with "These two coarses walk into a bar" is bad.

PHILIPPIANS

Philip means "Lover of Horses".   So Philippians means Equestrians.   And Equestrians are citizens of the ancient town of Equestra.   The Mayor of Equestra asked the Baker, "Tomorrow's my wife's birthday. Can you fill a cake order for me?" The Pastry Chef shook his head and said, "Alas, alas, my poor mayor. I cannot fill a cake. But I can fill a pie." And indeed he did; and henceforth, the city of Equestra became known as Fill-A-Pie. (A.k.a. Philippi.)

Birds of Prey?
No! Birds of Peace

From Philippians 1:7 (ESV):
for you are all partakers with me of grace

I even wore my reading glasses, but when I read that, for some "crazy" reason, I read the word partakers as parakeets. Thus, that passage came out: "for you are all parakeets with me of grace".

But if you think about it, the grace of Christ gives us wings, so I wasn't too far off. And if only we'd escape the cage of our sin and fly from the perch of our complacency, and somehow get outside the house of our earthly desires, we could fly free. But then we'd have to avoid the hawks of temptation and the owls of doubt. So let us devour the birdseed of the Gospel and chirp our songs of praise and thanksgiving.

Paul's "To Be Or Not to Be"* Soliloquy

Line from William Shakespeare's play "Hamlet".

Philippians 1:21-26
Paul talks about the pros and cons of

whether he lives or dies. Reminds me of Hamlet contemplating suicide. But I learned early on that if you say it sounds like Paul's contemplating suicide, the leader of the Bible Study will throw a holy hissy fit. While I mostly agree that Paul wasn't considering killing himself, I still feel someone supporting that assertion as adamantly as that Bible Study leader did, should offer a much more eloquent refutation than: Nuh-Uh!

You Can Say That Again

Philippians 3:1 & 4:4
In 3:1, Paul tells the Philippians to rejoice in the Lord and writes that it's not grievous nor tedious for him to write the same things again and again, because it's a safeguard for his readers. And to prove his point, in 4:4, he tells them to rejoice in the Lord always; and in the same verse, he again says rejoice. He's so happy to repeat himself, he even says "And again I say".

Maturity Comes with Age
... But Not Always

Philippians 3:15 (NIV):
All of us who are mature
should take such a view of things.
And if on some point you think differently,
that too God will make clear to you.

Sounds like a nice way of telling someone that they're not exactly right.

Some Are Six-Packs; Others Are Kegs

From Philippians 3:19 (NKJV):
whose god is their belly

Who wants to worship a god full of lint?
And how do you bow down to your belly?
Would losing weight lessen your god's
impact on your life? And would using The
Abdominizer strengthen it?

COLOSSIANS

Paul's Colossal Epistle to the church at
Colossae. The letter itself wasn't large, but Paul
wrote with such big letters. Colosse means
"Punishment, Correction", so imagine how happy
they were to hear about God's amazing grace!

Obtuse Obfuscation (a.k.a. Blah, Blah, Blah, Blah, Blah)

Colossians 2:8a (The Message):
Watch out for people who try to dazzle you
with big words and intellectual double-talk.

The longest word I found in the dictionary:
Pneumonoultramicroscopicsilicovolcanoconiosis.
Beware of people using that word to impress you.
For the record, I didn't use that word; I presented it.
I'm sure there's a difference.
Mostly sure.

"Thank You, Boss
for This Paperweight
with the Glowing Red Light"

Colossians 3:22 (ESV):
Slaves, obey in everything
those who are your earthly masters,
not by way of eye-service, as people-pleasers,
but with sincerity of heart, fearing the Lord.

Especially good advice nowadays when bosses sneak webcams wherever they please!

Ultimately, God is our Boss. And ultimately, He offers a much better retirement plan.

1 THESSALONIANS

Thessalonica means "Victory Against the Thessalians"; and since Thessalians sounds like people of Thistles, the Thessalonians must have been gwate weeders. They pwobably loved to weed and white too.

Zzzzzzzzzzz!

1 Thessalonians 4:14 (NASB):
For if we believe that Jesus died and rose again,
even so God will bring with Him
those who have fallen asleep in Jesus.

Does falling asleep in Jesus mean falling asleep listening to a sermon?

2 THESSALONIANS

If Thessalonians don't repent of their dirty ways, they'll become known as Messalonians.

Idle Worshippers

2 Thessalonians 3:11 (NIV):
We hear that some among you are idle. They are not busy; they are busybodies.

Idle-worshippers bow (or stretch out) in worship on their couches and beds.

1 TIMOTHY

Timothy means "Honoring God". Which means we should always be Timothying. Not just during hurricanes, heartaches, and various thundery. Timmying the night away.

Little Profit

1 Timothy 4:8a (NKJV):
For bodily exercise profits a little

In that case, I definitely overpaid for my gym membership.

**Having favorite Bible verses
is like having
antiperspirant for your soul
to help you not sweat the small stuff.**

"The Most Unkindest Cut of All"*

* Line from Shakespeare's play "Julius Caesar".

1 Timothy 5:8 (NASB):
But if anyone does not provide for his own,
and especially for those of his household,
he has denied the faith
and is worse than an unbeliever.

How can Paul create a worse insult for Christians? Unless he says, "You're worse than an unbeliever; you smell like a dog; and you walk like a duck."

2 TIMOTHY

Tim-Tim 2, the sequel, which hopefully answers all the questions raised by Timmy 1.

Crystal or Compost?
Choose Wisely!

2 Timothy 2:20-21 (The Message):
In a well-furnished kitchen
there are not only crystal goblets and silver platters,
but waste cans and compost buckets
—some containers used to serve fine meals,
others to take out the garbage.
Become the kind of container God can use
to present any and every kind of gift
to his guests for their blessing.

Yeah, what he said. Being a wine glass for God's better than being His spittoon. Or worse.

So That's Where Those Come From

2 Timothy 2:23 (NIV):
Don't have anything to do
with foolish and stupid arguments,
because you know they produce quarrels.

Be careful: If arguments create quarrels, they can also lead to squabbles and tiffs.

TITUS

Titus means "Honorable". But that name also refers to how a kidnapper kept his hostages from fleeing. "Why didn't you escape?" "He Titus." Or it could refer to a level of friendship. "Are you two close?" "We're Titus can be."

Cretans!

Titus 1:12-13a (NASB):
One of themselves, a prophet of their own, said,
"Cretans are always liars, evil beasts, lazy gluttons."
This testimony is true.

To clarify; that's not a compliment. Instead of lazy gluttons, the KJV says: "slow bellies". (Still not a compliment.) To make matters worse, Paul adds such insults are true!

PHILEMON

Philemon means "Loving, Friendly". Could also mean a male Jamaican file clerk. "What's his job in Jamaica?" "He's a Philemon."

Please Hear My Pleas

Philemon

Paul writes to fellow believer Philemon on behalf of his slave Onesimus. (Most church scholars agree Onesimus was a runaway slave who became a believer while on the run.) Paul "copies" two other believers on the letter, Apphia and Archippus, as well as the church that meets in Philemon's house. Martin Luther referred to Paul's complimentary opening as "holy flattery". And then Paul begins his plea for Onesimus, calling him his son, a beloved brother, and his heart. Paul makes a pun! The name Onesimus means useful. So Paul says that Onesimus was useless before, but now has become useful to both Philemon and Paul. Onesimus also means beneficial, so Paul makes another pun when he says he wants some benefits from Philemon in the Lord. Thus, he makes two puns for the price of one.

Paul says he's sending Onesimus back, but writes he would rather keep him, saying although he could make commands in the name of Christ, he prefers instead to make heartfelt appeals. He states his keeping Onesimus would be like Onesimus taking Philemon's place in helping Paul. How heartfelt can you get?

Paul wheels and deals! He plays the Age Card in a subtle, though definitive, Respect Your Elders sort of way when he refers to himself as an old man. Next, he plays the Chain Card. That card trumps most others. Paul reminds Philemon how he is in prison, in chains, for preaching the Gospel. Even better, the Gospel Chain Card! He also asserts Onesimus is Philemon's brother in the Lord.

He tells Philemon whatever Onesimus owes him, Philemon should charge to Paul, so Paul will owe Philemon instead of Onesimus. In the NKJV, Paul uses his famous phrase "not to mention", which he also uses in 2 Corinthians 9:4. His wry way of slipping in some humor to make his point. Where upon Paul reminds Philemon he owes Paul for the everlasting security of his eternal soul! The I Saved Your Soul Card! Paul plays a mighty hand indeed.

He closes saying he's confident Philemon will heed his request; and adds this caveat: He hopes to visit soon. I.e., he'll check on Philemon to see how he treated Onesimus. Thus, ensuring a win with the I'll Be Watching You Card.

Paul's so convincing I'm sure Philemon complies with his wishes. Maybe Paul's powers of persuasion are why people rob Peter to pay him.

HEBREWS

Hebrews means a man makes coffee. Or whatever else a man might brew.

Lissssstennnnn Carefullllllyyyyyyy

Hebrews 5:11 (NIV):
We have much to say about this,
but it is hard to explain
because you are slow to learn.

Sounds like someone's headed for Summer School. Again!

Do You Swear to Tell the Truth?
Naw, I Just Swear When I'm Mad

Hebrews 6:13
When God made a promise to Abraham, He had to swear by Himself, since no one's greater than God. Like when "God" takes the witness stand in the courtroom to testify in the 1977 movie "Oh, God!" and says: "I swear to tell the truth, the whole truth, and nothing but the truth, so help Me, Me."

Gird Up Your Loins

Hebrews 7:9-10 (NKJV):
Even Levi, who receives tithes,
paid tithes through Abraham, so to speak,
for he was still in the loins of his father
when Melchizedek met him.

Ha! In that case, we were all in Adam's loins when he sinned. Ohhhhhh. That's what's meant by original sin. I thought "original sin" meant a clever new way to behave badly. Like dating Siamese twins on the Sabbath. Behind each other's back. While eating stolen undercooked pork!

JAMES

Informally known as Jimmy.
Or Jim for short.

I Can't Remember What I Look Like!

James 1:23-24 (NIV):
Anyone who listens to the word
but does not do what it says
is like a man who looks at his face in a mirror and,
after looking at himself, goes away
and immediately forgets what he looks like.

"Do I have red hair and green eyes? I can't remember! I'm sure I'm a tanned, muscular man." (Finds mirror, screams in horror.) "Aw, man! I look like that? No wonder I drove that image out of my mind. Just so I can step outside during the day, I'm gonna need a radioactive shield!"

I Hope You Feel Better; Take Care of Yourself; and Have a Nice Day!

James 2:14-17
To illustrate how faith without works is dead, James cites how merely telling someone who

is naked and hungry to be warm and fed without providing any clothes or food is useless. And so, a deedless faith is a dead faith. Reminds me of the fictional public service announcement from the 2009-2010 ABC show "Better Off Ted" which said: "The Veridian Dynamics Foundation: Helping the world. By telling people we're helping the world."
No matter what problems you face, I hope you feel better. Don't forget to take care of yourself. And have a nice day! Doesn't my hoping you feel better make you feel so much better? Wouldn't freshly-baked chocolate chip cookies accomplish so much more? How can you go wrong with chocolate? Unless you're helping someone overcome obesity or deal with diabetes.

Oh, No! Dudley Didn't Do Right?

James 4:17 (NASB):
Therefore, to one who knows the right thing to do and does not do it, to him it is sin.

Sins of Omission? You've got to be kidding me! That's like taxes. Not only do they tax you when you make money; they tax you when you spend it too. They get you coming and going. Same thing here. Not only do you get in trouble when you do wrong; you get in trouble when you don't do right. Coming and going, they get you! If that's the way it is, the only way we'll get to Heaven is by God's grace.
Oh. Thank You Lord!

The concept of getting in trouble for what we don't do reminds me of what comedian, writer, and actor Damon Wayans said: "My friend Larry's in jail now. He got twenty-five years for something he didn't do. He didn't run fast enough."

I Want Patience; and I Want It Now!

James 5:11b (NCV):
You have heard about Job's patience,
and you know the Lord's purpose
for him in the end.
You know the Lord is full of mercy and is kind.

I prayed for the patience of Job one time. One time. That was the only time in my life, I ever got a boil. So I'll never do that again.

Now I pray for the patience of Bill Gates and Warren Buffet.

Cha-Ching!

**Why do people pray
for me to have patience,
instead of praying for God
to give me what I want right now?!**

1 PETER

Peter means "Rock". Which sounds tough; right? But poor Paul; his name means "small". And yet everyone robs Rocky to pay Small.

Do You Know Who Built the Ark?
No. Uhhh.
That's Right!

Excerpt from 1 Peter 3:20 (NIV):
God waited patiently in the days of Noah
while the ark was being built

Noah's grandfather was Methuselah. His claim to fame is living the longest. To show how patient God is, even during His Old Testament Days, the name Methuselah means: "When he dies, it will come." It? What it? The Flood! Methuselah lived 969 years. Long before electricity, cable TV, and the Internet, so that was a lonnnnnnggggggg time. They didn't even have air conditioning! Their 'lions, tigers, and bears, oh my'* weren't in zoos. When they handfed them, they used their hands!

For 969 lonnnnnnnggggggg years, God waited patiently before sending the Flood. Eventually the Flood's alarm clock went off; and that kind of clock doesn't come with a snooze button.

Nothing matters more than the eternal salvation of your soul. Not even (gulp!) chocolate, money, or supermodels. Those things won't last. Except for the souls of the supermodels. So give your soul to Jesus now. Don't let your life turn out to be a losing game of Trivial Pursuit.

*Line from the 1939 movie "The Wizard of Oz".

2 PETER

Peter means a person who petes. As in peat moss.

They Say That Balaam's One Bad Connoisseur

2 Peter 2:15-19 (The Message):
They've left the main road and are directionless,
having taken the way of Balaam, son of Beor,
the prophet who turned profiteer,
a connoisseur of evil.
But Balaam was stopped in his wayward tracks:
A dumb animal spoke in a human voice
and prevented the prophet's craziness.
There's nothing to these people
—they're dried-up fountains,
storm-scattered clouds,
headed for a black hole in hell.
They are loudmouths, full of hot air,
but still they're dangerous.
Men and women who have recently escaped
from a deviant life
are most susceptible to their brand of seduction.
They promise these newcomers freedom,
but they themselves are slaves of corruption,
for if they're addicted to corruption
—and they are—they're enslaved.

I like the alliterative phrasings, such as "the prophet who turned profiteer."

The reference to Balaam's donkey as a "dumb animal" reminds me of Brian Regan's routine where he talks about driving down the road and seeing a truck pulling a horse trailer with a sign which read: "Caution: Transporting Show Horses." So Brian puts his hands at ten and two on his steering wheel to drive as carefully as he can. "These horses have to put on a show!" Later, he passes another truck pulling a trailer, but its sign says: "Don't Worry: Just Dumb Old Donkeys." So he crosses the line and bumps the trailer a couple times with his car. "Who cares? Just dumb old donkeys. They refused to apply themselves."

1 JOHN

John again! His name still means whatever it meant before. He wrote five books of the Bible, four of which bear his name! Paul wrote more books than that, but he didn't name any after himself.

What's going on with John? Billing himself as the Beloved Disciple. Pointing out that he beat Peter in a race to the tomb. Having his Mommy ask if he and his brother James can sit on each side of Jesus in Heaven. I don't understand how he can have abandonment issues, when he's the one who abandoned his father. Not the other way around.

To John's credit though, Jesus entrusted His Mother to his care. So I can't complain about him, nor should I try.

Yep, Darkness'll Do That to a Person

1 John 2:11 (NCV):
But whoever hates a brother or sister is in darkness,
lives in darkness, and does not know where to go,
because the darkness has made that person blind.

Darkness will make you blind! At least,
back in the days before flashlights with Eveready
batteries. Which reminds me, when it comes to the
Lord's return, we too should be Eveready.

And That's No Lie!

1 John 2:21b (NASB):
no lie is of the truth.

I'm glad John cleared that up for me.

"Right On!"*

* *Hip phrase from the 1960s and 70s.*

From 1 John 3:7 (NASB):
the one who practices righteousness is righteous

The one who practices wrongeousness is
wrongeous. And the one who practices middle-of-
the-roadeousness is middle-of-the-roadeous.

<u>2 JOHN</u>

John-John.

Stay with the Group!

2 John 9 (NIV):
Anyone who runs ahead
and does not continue in the teaching of Christ
does not have God;
whoever continues in the teaching
has both the Father and the Son.

"Anyone who runs ahead."   Are we first graders on a field trip? Okay, in many ways we are. We love to get out of class. We can't sit still on the bus. Silence and single file are out of the question. We want what the other person has for snack. And we miss our mommies.

3 JOHN

John-John-John.

The Battle of the Ds:

That Diotrephes Is Bad News ...

3 John 9-10 (ESV):
I have written something to the church,
but Diotrephes, who likes to put himself first,
does not acknowledge our authority.
So if I come, I will bring up what he is doing,
talking wicked nonsense against us.
And not content with that, he refuses to
welcome the brothers, and also stops those
who want to and puts them out of the church.

Owing to his spouting wicked nonsense, he obviously flunked citizenship. His report cards read: "Doesn't get along well with others."

... But That Demetrius Is A-Okay

3 John 12 (The Message):
Everyone has a good word for Demetrius
—the Truth itself stands up for Demetrius!
We concur, and you know
we don't hand out endorsements lightly.

He got As in citizenship. "Plays well with others and shares."

**Is one who concurs
a concurer?**

JUDE

Hey! Jude*, a variation of Judah, means "Praise". And people who praise are generally joyful. Thus, Jude could be considered a contraction for the phrase: Joyful Dude. As in Hey Joyful Dude, 'don't make it bad'*.

Title and line from the 1968 Beatles' song "Hey Jude" written by John Lennon & Paul McCartney.

I Changed My Mind

Jude 3 (NCV):
Dear friends, I wanted very much to write you about the salvation we all share.

But I felt the need to write you
about something else:
I want to encourage you to fight hard for the faith
that was given the holy people of God
once and for all time.

Jude wanted to write about the salvation we share, but felt compelled to encourage us to fight for our faith. Surely Jude could "take a sad song and make it better."* "Na-na-na-na-na-na-na!"*

From "Hey Jude" written by Lennon/McCartney.

Shungodly*

Jude 14-15 (NIV) (**Emphasis** added):
Enoch, the seventh from Adam, prophesied
about these men: "See, the Lord is coming
with thousands upon thousands of his holy ones
to judge everyone, and to convict all the **ungodly**
of all the **ungodly** acts they have done
in the **ungodly** way, and of all the harsh words
ungodly sinners have spoken against him."

Can't blame Enoch for excessive repetition. They didn't have thesauruses back then. Or if they did; they didn't have as many words as we do.

* The ungodly shun God; thus, they're shungodly.

**Preachers always tell us not to sin.
But Jesus didn't sin;
and look what happened to Him.**

REVELATION
(a.k.a. The Revelation of Jesus Christ)

Revelation means a divine disclosure. A reveal-ation of God's will. Everybody sing!: "You say you want a revelation; well, you know, we all want to hear the Lord."*

My spoof of the 1968 Beatles' song "Revolution" written by John Lennon and Paul McCartney.

What an Appealing Apocalypse

Revelation 6:13-14 (NCV):
And the stars in the sky fell to the earth
like figs falling from a fig tree
when the wind blows.
The sky disappeared as a scroll when it is rolled up,
and every mountain and island
was moved from its place.

With figs falling from a tree and a scroll rolling up, John uses such delicate imagery for the destruction of this Earth. Granted the Tribulation Period will be full of turmoil, but it sounds so poetic when John describes it.

Your head will be severed from your body like a precious pebble tumbling down a daisy-covered hill amidst the fluttering of butterfly wings.

**It's no puzzle!
When battling Satan,
use cross words.**

Sweet and Sour Scroll

Revelation 10:9-10 (NCV):
So I went to the angel
and told him to give me the small scroll.
And he said to me,
"Take the scroll and eat it.
It will be sour in your stomach,
but in your mouth it will be sweet as honey."
So I took the small scroll
from the angel's hand and ate it.
In my mouth it tasted sweet as honey,
but after I ate it, it was sour in my stomach.

I could see if it tasted so sweet, he overate and got sick to his stomach. Or, if like Baker's chocolate, it looked sweet, but tasted bitter.

So I guess the proper approach for enjoying tasty scrolls is to adopt the method of those who chew tobacco. Suck on the scroll to savor its flavor, and then spit it out, so you don't get sick. And by all means, don't step in it.

An Important Point
Most Christians Miss

Revelation 13:18
The number of the Beast is 666! While trying to determine who the Beast is, most Christians fail to realize that if the Beast dangles upside-down or stands on his head, his number becomes 999.

Ribbit! Ribbit! Ribbit!
Talk about Demonic Bad Breath!

Revelation 16:13-14a (NASB):
And I saw coming out of the mouth of the dragon
and out of the mouth of the beast
and out of the mouth of the false prophet,
three unclean spirits like frogs;
for they are spirits of demons

Regardless of what their commercials say,
no toothpaste and no breath mint can rid you of that
stench.

Instead, try gargling with the Gospel.

No Matter How Cutie,
Don't Be the Nudie
Who Gets Kicked Out of the Wedding

Revelation 19:7-8 (NIV):
Let us rejoice and be happy
and give him [God] glory,
because the wedding of the Lamb has come,
and the Lamb's bride has made herself ready.
Fine linen, bright and clean,
was given to her to wear."
(The fine linen means the good things
done by God's holy people.)

Here's the joyous celebration where Jesus
marries his bride, the fellowship of true believers.
But a wedding shouldn't be a blind date. We need

to connect with Jesus, get to know Him first. Even Jesus doesn't want to marry a Mail-Order Bride.

My uncle ordered a mail-order bride from Czechoslovakia. After three weeks, he asked why she hadn't arrived yet. And that company assured him, "The Czech's in the mail!"

**Judgment Day is when
The Great Carpenter returns
and brings The Hammer down.**

A New World Order?

Revelation 21:4b (NIV):
There will be no more death
or mourning or crying or pain,
for the old order of things has passed away.

No more death, mourning, crying, or pain sounds good. Does the Bible end with a Big Finish? A Grand Finale that garners lots of laughs and thunderous applause? Yes!

Many kinds of laughter exist. We mostly laugh at something incongruous. But we also laugh when nervous. Or better yet, when overjoyed.

When you know Jesus as your Lord and Savior and recognize the everlasting joy only He can give, your heart can be filled with laughter too. And that's my prayer for you.

I also pray that if you have chocolate, you'll share. :o)

THE ULTIMATE MOVIE TRAILER!

(To be read with a Movie Announcer's voice):

In a world, where mankind has been sold into sin, The Only Begotten Son of God will leave His Throne of Glory in Heaven to become The One Man Who will fulfill The Righteous Law of God.

He will be betrayed by a close friend. Convicted of a crime He did not commit. He will make The Ultimate Sacrifice to save the One He Loves. He Alone will pay the price for our sins, shedding His Holy and Innocent Blood to set free those who repent and believe.

When His dead body is buried, His arch nemesis will cackle with delight, while His loved ones will weep. But when all seems lost, His friends will rejoice; and His enemies will weep, when, on the third day, as foretold long ago, He will rise from the dead, defeating sin, death, and the devil.

After forty days, He will ascend into Heaven and send His Holy Spirit to comfort and guide us, helping us share His Love with others.

And if you believe this is The Greatest Story Ever Told, wait until you experience the joy and rapture of the sequel: "Jesus 2: Return of the King."

Coming soon.

To a Judgment Day near you.

PARTING THOUGHTS

Thank you for joining me on this joyful journey of jocularity. I hope you had a blest blast. Here are the answers to the Questions to Ponder from page 8:

● Which animal did Christian musician David Meece call "the original Mister Ed"? -- Balaam's talking donkey in Numbers 22. You can learn more about David Meece at: www.davidmeece.com

● Who said (in the RSV): "Do I lack madmen, that you have brought this fellow to play the madman in my presence?" -- The Philistine king Achish in 1 Samuel 21:10-15.

● Which book of the Bible do I say is like a textbook on how to write a great comedy? -- Esther.

● What's so funny about a handkerchief? -- Means sweat rag. See the explanation for Luke 19:11-27.

And more importantly:

● What makes a great gift for birthdays, confirmation, Easter, Thanksgiving, Christmas, anytime? -- You're reading it!

● What about "The Crosscheck Cookie (or Bun or Carrot) Game"? -- At least seven! Pages 119, 125, 130, 149, 152, 167, and 198. If you really really like cookies (or buns or carrots); and seven's not enough, you could include pages 8, 153, and 173.

I'm not suggesting the Bible is a book of humor. It's historical, not hysterical. His Story. The thrust and theme of which are Salvation and Redemption in Jesus. A Divinely Romantic Love Story where the Hero dies a brutal death to win back the one He loves. But Praise the Lord. He comes back to life! And He and His newfound Bride live Happily Ever After. Or that is, we will, when He returns for us.

I wanted to keep the book "light", since the focus is on Holy Laughter! So I avoided being dogmatic as much as possible. But I'd feel remiss if I wrote a book about the Bible without giving you the Main Message of the Bible: The Gospel. The Good News about Jesus!

Although the Bible contains humor, the Lord speaks seriously about sin. Unfortunately, the Devil, the present world, and our own sinful natures pull us away from the wonderful plan God has for our lives. God is holy and cannot tolerate evil. And yet, all of us have sinned! But God loves us and want us to be with Him. So what's a Holy and Loving Divine Being to do?

If He stays true to His Holiness, none of us can enter His Presence; God ends up alone; and we wind up in misery, being separated from His Love for all eternity, but if He stays true to His Love and lets everyone into Heaven no matter what, His Justice and Holiness get destroyed; He violates His Divine Nature. Which would probably end all existence as we know it. But not in a good way.

What if God punishes sin to satisfy His Justice, but does so in a way that allows us to survive the aftermath. That means we can't pay the price for our own sins. We can't become "good enough" on our own. But if Someone Holy, Someone Innocent, pays the penalty, that would work. Since none of us are holy or innocent, God must pay the price Himself. And so, He did.

God became the God-Man Jesus, lived a perfect life, and fulfilled the requirements of His Holy Law. And then, He died on the cross to shed His Holy and Innocent Blood to pay for our sins. To keep us from wondering whether Jesus' Sacrifice was sufficient, Jesus rose from the dead on the third day. After forty days, He ascended into Heaven to sit at the right hand of God the Father, to plead on our behalf against the accusations of the Devil. Ten days later, Jesus sent us the Holy Spirit.

In response, we must repent of our unbelief and disobedience and believe God loves us so much He sent His Only Begotten Son Jesus to die for us, so those who believe in Jesus will not suffer eternal separation from God, but will enjoy everlasting life in Heaven. For God didn't send Jesus to condemn us, but to reconcile us to Him, for Jesus is The Way, The Truth, and The Life; and no one comes to God the Father, except through repentance and faith in Jesus. (John 3:16-17 and 14:6.)

What else should we do? Pray to God the Father in the Name of God the Son: Jesus, ask the Holy Spirit to guide us, declare our faith in Jesus as our Only Hope of Salvation, love one another, even our enemies, forgive others, ask for forgiveness too, give thanks for our many blessings, be generous as we bless others, and continue to read God's Word. All of God's Word, not just the funny parts, but thank you for letting me share those with you.

Because of Adam's fall into sin, we're born dead. Spiritually dead. Most dead people don't know they're dead. Spiritually dead people anyway. Like Haley Joel Osment said as Cole Sears in the 1999 movie "The Sixth Sense": "I see dead people. Walking around like regular people. They only see what they want to see. They don't know they're dead." Corpses can't save themselves. When we're dead, we can't bring ourselves back to life. Thus. Ergo. Therefore. (Pick your favorite.) **Christianity isn't a crutch; it's a defibrillator!** Not a walking stick for someone wounded, nor help for someone hurt. But ZAP!!! Resuscitation. To bring a dead man back to life. I hope that makes everything: CLEAR!

Thank you! God bless you! And remember, The Creator of the Universe is crazy about you. The tormentor of the universe is crazy at you. There's a difference. A big difference!

Jesus loves you.
The Devil hates you.
I just wanna be friends.

Blessings & Joy,
Dean

Made in the USA
Columbia, SC
04 August 2023